THE EMPTY CORE

"In this superb book, Dr. Seinfeld begins by offering the reader a brilliant overview of the British object relations school. . . . He then demonstrates the useful application of the theory of the empty core via vivid and beautifully written case material, case material that is so real that the reader is drawn into the therapeutic process. Here his interpretations are often dazzling in their directness and accuracy, yet these often bold interpretations are always respectful, well timed, and empathic. . . . It is rare to find a book that combines meticulous scholarship with originality and energy of such a high order. *The Empty Core* is a brilliant and exciting book."

—Diana Siskind, CSW

"This is an exciting book. Not only is it exciting from the point of giving a clear exposition of object relations theory, but also in terms of the author's ability to use case material to show you how to use the theory. Few books share clinical case material with such freedom, clarity, and instruction. Dr. Seinfeld revolutionizes the way clinical material is listened to and how the clinician responds. He gives the reader a step-by-step description of how he responds to the patient's self states. He enables the reader to understand and speak to the subjective worldview and self states of the patient with interpretations that are completely object relational. He speaks the language of the patient's affective reality, thereby conveying a genuine capacity to understand the unmet relational needs and wishes of the child within the patient."

—Robert S. Berger, MS, CSW

"Jeffrey Seinfeld's *The Empty Core* is a welcome addition to the current dialogue on the origins and functions of 'emptiness.' He explores the empty core of the schizoid personality, and helps the clinician to see how work with the latter differs from work with the borderline personalities. . . .

"Seinfeld's palette includes the British school, Sartre, and Lacan, but also American ego and self psychologies. His writing is not polemical or divisive. He shows how different schools relate to his concerns, and he does this very well. The Independent British school of psychoanalysis is his home base and main source of his insights. What is especially important is his emphasis on Fairbairn, whose work has not received the attention it deserves in this country. Seinfeld helps redress this wrong and shows the importance of Fairbairn's understanding of schizoid phenomena for clinical work today. . . .

"Seinfeld gives many clinical illustrations in a clearly written way, so that the mental health workers can follow what he does in a step-by-step fashion, and apply his work to their own cases. . . . The book brims with useful clinical hints."

—Michael Eigen, Ph.D.

THE EMPTY CORE

An Object Relations Approach to Psychotherapy of the Schizoid Personality

JEFFREY SEINFELD, PH.D.

JASON ARONSON INC.
Northvale, New Jersey
London

Production Editor: Bernard F. Horan
Editorial Director: Muriel Jorgensen

This book was set in 12 point Bem
by Lind Graphics of Upper Saddle River, New Jersey,
and printed and bound by Haddon Craftsmen of Scranton, Pennsylvania.

Library of Congress Cataloging-in-Publication Data

Seinfeld, Jeffrey.
    The empty core : an object relations approach to psychotherapy of the
schizoid personality / Jeffrey Seinfeld.
        p.   cm.
    Includes bibliographical references and index.
    ISBN 0-87668-611-0
    1. Schizophrenia—Treatment.   2. Object relations (Psychoanalysis)
3. Psychotherapy.   I. Title.
    [DNLM: 1. Psychotherapy.   2. Schizoid Personality Disorder.
3. Schizoid Personality Disorder—therapy.   WM 203 S461e]
RC514.S424   1991
616.89'80651—dc20
DNLM/DLC
for Library of Congress   90-14534

Manufactured in the United States of America. Jason Aronson Inc. offers books
and cassettes. For information and catalog write to Jason Aronson Inc., 230
Livingston Street, Northvale, New Jersey 07647.

Dedicated to my mother
and the memory of my father

Contents

Preface

Psychoanalytic contributions in America have focused much attention upon the borderline and narcissistic personality disorders. This important emphasis has been at the expense of the third severe personality disorder, the schizoid condition. The relative neglect of the schizoid disorder is surprising, given that in the literature, this condition is considered the most common of the serious personality disorders. In fact, in British object relations theory, the schizoid position is the core of the personality structure, and schizoid states are present and fundamental in all psychopathology.

In his original and outstanding work, W. R. D. Fairbairn, one of the pioneering founders of object relations theory, presented much of what is known about schizoid states. He asserted that schizoid patients, by the experience of early rejection, had been made afraid to love. Schizoid patients are usually thought to be visibly withdrawn, affectively isolated, marginally functional, and behaviorally eccentric. However, these patients may sometimes be misdiagnosed because they do not fit the typical description of withdrawal from interpersonal relations and social situations. Schizoid patients may role-play at relationships and social involvement, relating in accord with a stereotyped idea of how to behave as a wife, husband, lover, friend, or colleague without genuine emotional involvement. Furthermore, seemingly neurotic, narcissistic, or borderline patients may suffer from an underlying schizoid core. The treatment of these patients can reach an impasse because the therapeutic interventions appropriate for other personality disorders may be ineffective in the treatment of schizoid phenomena.

This book is first and foremost a clinical approach to psychotherapy of the schizoid states; in addition, the idea of the empty core as a framework for the schizoid position is introduced. There is a discussion of differential diagnosis with the borderline condition, and clinical vignettes illustrate how the therapist responds to the schizoid false self, with detailed discussion of interventions addressed to antisocial behavior and the fear of engulfment. The book shows how the therapist may relate playfully to the patient's use of transitional objects and how to "hold" the patient through therapeutic regression.

In treatment, the schizoid patient typically creates an invisible wall between himself and the therapist. This emotional distance protects him from establishing dependence upon a human object relationship. The schizoid person experiences his object relationship needs as insatiable, destructive, even vampirish. Thus, to shield himself and the therapist, he painfully swallows his object hunger. However, the warding off of relational needs increases their intensity and urgency. The schizoid patient does not accept the therapist's empathy because his sense of self is so fragile and vulnerable that any contact is dreaded as an impingement on this secret self.

The purpose of this volume is to show how to overcome one of the greatest obstacles to psychotherapy—the schizoid dread of potentially good object relations. The reader is shown how to reach out and contact the patient's vulnerable self and to create a holding environment that respects the patient's need for distance while, paradoxically, helping him to become involved in a human relationship. In addition, some of the rather poetical concepts of object relations theory that describe schizoid phenomena—the secret self, the transformational object, the basic fault—are made to come alive through case vignettes that illustrate their value in clinical intervention. Chapters are also presented on child therapy, substance abuse by the schizoid personality, and countertransference reactions.

Acknowledgment

I would like to express my gratitude to my wife, Rhonda, and my daughter, Leonora, for their support and encouragement.

I would like to thank Jason Aronson, M.D., and his editorial staff for their invaluable support and assistance. Dean Shirley Ehrenkranz, Dr. George Frank, Dr. Eda Goldstein, Dr. Burt Shachter, and Dr. Gladys Gonzalez-Ramos of the New York University School of Social Work were important sources of inspiration, encouragement, and collegiality. My thanks goes to Mrs. Pat Nitzburg and Mrs. Rita Smith of the Jewish Board of Family and Children's Services for their staunch and unwavering support. I am grateful to Mr. Robert Berger, Ms. Theresa Aiello-Gerber, Dr. Michael Gropper, Ms. Jane Charna Meyers, Dr. Martin Schulman, and Dr. Gerald Schoenewolf for their friendship, encouragement, and support. I am grateful to Ms. Jeanetta Bushey, Ms. Cheri Lieberman, Ms. Karen Wexler, and Ms. Gail Talcoff for the contribution of case material. I thank Ms. Hana Melnik for her excellent ideas. Mr. Richard Lenert has provided me with excellent secretarial help.

1

A FRAMEWORK FOR THE EMPTY CORE

The term *schizoid* refers to the splitting of the self. The schizoid individual complains of feeling isolated, disengaged, shut-out, unconnected, and apathetic. There is a consuming need for object dependence but attachment threatens the schizoid with the loss of self. The individual protects an insecure sense of self by emotional withdrawal and affective isolation. Unable to make emotionally meaningful commitments, the person often feels that life is futile and without purpose (Meissner 1988). Existential phenomenology describes the schizoid sense of identity as suffering ontological insecurity (Laing 1959). The schizoid frequently has few friends, is not involved with community or society in general, and may appear shy and eccentric. There may be paranoid features: sensitivity, guardedness, suspiciousness (Meissner 1988).

The schizoid may also seem to be sociable and involved in relationships. However, he is frequently playing a role and not fully involved, unconsciously disowning this role (Fairbairn 1940). Winnicott (1960) described the false-self system.

3

The schizoid personality maintains a compliant and protective facade to shield a fragile sense of inner autonomy and individuation from intimate contact with the object. The false self protects the true self from losing its subjectivity and vitality (Eigen 1986). The schizoid may also develop a variant of the false-self system, an as-if personality. The individual relates to the object world on the basis of childlike imitation, expressing a superficial identification with the environment but with a lack of genuine warmth (Meissner 1988). The as-if structure serves to defend against the underlying schizoid emptiness and sense of futility. The values and convictions of the as-if personality tend toward identification with whatever individual or group the person finds at the time.

The schizoid person presents as superficial, concrete, overly related to facticity and reality (Giovacchini 1986). Despite the constriction and repression of phantasy life, he may on occasion reveal strange and fantastic dream fragments or fleeting segments of phantasy suggesting a rich and complex inner world. (British object relations analysts have been inclined to use *phantasy* in referring to unconscious phantasy and *fantasy* to refer to the conscious level of such psychic activity.) The affect is constricted. The schizoid withdraws from the external world in favor of a preoccupation with internal life. As long as one can successfully repress intense dependence, the schizoid functions well in the real world. The character structure and defenses remain stable but rigid.

FAIRBAIRN AND THE SCHIZOID CONDITION

A half-century ago, Fairbairn (1940) presented his work on the schizoid personality. Most of what is known about schizoid phenomena can be found in this classic essay and the four that followed. These papers introduced a complete object relations theory of the personality (Fairbairn 1941, 1943, 1944, 1946).

The schizoid patient has withdrawn from disappointing external object relations into the imaginary internal world of bad objects described as exciting (but nongratifying), enticing, bewitching, addicting, rejecting, persecuting, and punishing. There is a constant interplay between the introjection of external objects and the projection of internal objects. Depressive and borderline states result from the fear of object loss based on the hating, destructive wishes toward the object. Schizoid anxiety is centered on the fear that one's love destroys the object (Fairbairn 1940). Ogden (1989) states, "Since we are dealing with the earliest human relationship, that of mother and infant, the notion of the infant's love should be understood as virtually synonymous with the infant's way of being with and needing the mother" (p. 87).

The Schizoid Position

In the British object relations psychoanalytic discourse, the term schizoid refers not only to a specific pathological personality disorder but also to the foundation of psychic structure. Fairbairn (1944) posits that in a theoretically ideal state of nature, the relationship between infant and mother would be perfectly satisfactory. Therefore, there would be no libidinal frustration and no ambivalence on the part of the infant toward the primary object. While aggression is considered a primary dynamic factor in itself and therefore not resolvable into libido, it remains subordinate to libido. The infant's aggression toward the object is viewed as a response to frustration and not a spontaneously arising feeling. The infant is separated from the primary caregiver by the realities of modern times before the child is naturally disposed to separate from the mother's care. The question of whether aggression is innate or a response to frustration becomes purely academic because perfect conditions do not exist in the reality of our contemporary society. The infant with these circumstances splits off and internalizes the frustrating components of the object and the corresponding self states. A more or less ideal relationship exists with external reality while the inner world is comprised of addictive but non-gratifying and persecutory object relations. Fairbairn (1944) designates this internal object world "the endopsychic situation" (p. 82).

Fairbairn's reference to an ideal state of nature is based on the social philosophy of Rousseau (1762). As Wilson (1988) points out, Rousseau influenced the novelist Charles Dickens, who portrayed innocent youth corrupted by modern industrial civilization. The romantic views of Rousseau and Dickens were a part of the culture in which the British psychoanalytic object relations authors were born and bred. Concepts such as the perfect state of nature and the true and false self grew out of this soil. Fairbairn cannot be considered a pure idealist because he is convinced that perfect object relations between the primary caregiver and infant are not achievable. There is a difference here between his views and those of the American psychoanalytic dialogue. American ego psychology and even self psychology would agree that disappointments in early object relations are inevitable but would contend that if not traumatic, the disappointments are necessary for growth and result in strengthening ego functions (Hartmann 1950) and transmuting internalizations (Kohut 1977). Fairbairn believes that in an ideally secure holding state, the infant would not require externally situated disruption to separate and individuate but would spontaneously do so, although at a later time.

In Fairbairn's early theory, the inner world was completely pathological in the sense of consisting entirely of badobject relations. In his later views, he postulated an ideal good object but portrayed the endopsychic structure as fully formed. Therefore, he never described the dynamics of the development of a good object (object constancy) in relation to the surrounding bad object world. I described the development of object constancy in relation to Fairbairn's inner world of bad objects and presented a dynamic model of the negative therapeutic reaction in borderline states (1990).

Emptiness

The infant needs to be loved as a person in its own right. Thus, the infant is object related. Libidinal pleasure serves as a signpost to the object (Fairbairn 1944). The infant's need to be loved is expressed as oral need, sucking, the wish for holding, comforting, and recognition. The caregiver's unsatisfactory response to the infant or the infant's incapacity to extract from the caregiver may have to do with a failure to love on the part of the primary object but it could also have to do with many other factors having little or nothing to do with love. The infant experiences all failures to respond to the need to be loved as a rejection. Fairbairn is strictly outlining the subjective view of the infant, in stating that the child comes to feel that he is not loved, that his love for the object is neither accepted nor valued. He begins to view the caregiver as a bad object for not loving him, that his love directed outward is bad (destructive). To keep his love as good and as pure as possible, he directs it inward. The child concludes that love relationships are bad (destructive) and therefore not to be trusted.

The deprivation of love is felt as emptiness. Being loved is felt as fullness. The physiological experience of emptiness associated with hunger becomes a metaphor and the basis of a psychic state of emptiness associated with the lack of love. Deprivation and emptiness enlarge the incorporative field: the need to incorporate the contents of the breast becomes the need to incorporate the breast itself and then even the mother as a whole. I suggest that the experience of emptiness becomes the empty core of psychic structure. The empty core is the sense of lack or fissure in a primitive, sensory-dominated, pre-symbolic state of boundedness more primitive than the internal object world. Ogden (1989) describes the autistic/ contiguous position as the underbelly of the schizoid position. He states:

> The autistic/contiguous mode is conceptualized as a sensory-dominated, pre-symbolic mode of generating experience which provides a good measure of the boundedness of human experience, and the beginning of a sense of the place where one's experience occurs. Anxiety in this mode consists of an unspeakable terror of the dissolution of boundedness resulting in feelings of leaking, falling, or dissolving into endless, shapeless spaces. [p. 81]

The empty core is the endless, shapeless space that arises as a minus or lack in boundedness and threatens the dissolution of being and boundedness. In existential phenomenology, the empty core is referred to as nothingness. Fairbairn (1944) contends that libido is the signpost to the object that instinctual drives are object related. I understand him to mean that instinctual drives are not complete in themselves but create, in the individual, a need for something external; they embody a sense of incompletion and lack. In existential phenomenology, it is a sense of incompletion or lack that is described as nothingness, a hole in the plentitude of being (Sartre 1943).

In the British object relations viewpoint, the erotogenic zones are not innately programmed biologically but become libidinalized because they provide the least resistance to the object and can serve the theme of internalization of the object. Sartre (1984) presents a strikingly similar view eloquently:

> The Freudians rightly saw that the innocent action of the child who plays at digging holes was not so innocent at all

nor that which consists in sliding one's finger into some hole in a door or wall. They relate it to fecal pleasures which children take in being given or administered enemas and they weren't wrong. But the core of the matter remains unclear: Must all such experiences be reduced to the sole experience of anal pleasure? . . . In other words, Freud will consider that all holes, for which the child, are symbolic anuses which attract him as a function of that kinship, whereas for my part I wonder whether the anus is not, in the child, an object of lust because it is a hole . . . the world is a kingdom of holes. I see, in fact, that the hole is bound up with refusal, with negation and nothingness. The hole is first and foremost what is not. [pp. 149–150]

From an object relations perspective, the erotogenic zones lend themselves to serving as signifiers of the infant's need for an object. Fairbairn (1941) suggests that they become libidinalized because they are the paths of least resistance to the object or lend themselves to the metaphor of incorporation.

The Empty Core, Need, and Desire

Fairbairn's pioneering work on the unsatisfactory experience with the object, emptiness, and the internalization of the object was far ahead of his time, but sometimes did not follow through on all of its implications. I shall therefore develop theory where Fairbairn left off and propose the theory of the empty core. I suggest that biological needs engender a sense of lack that becomes the empty core. The physiological state of emptiness resulting from hunger is translated into a psychic state of emptiness that becomes the core of psychic structure. The empty core is felt as a lack disrupting the sense of boundedness or wholeness. The empty core is not a static space. It is the hunger for objects internal and external. It is a state of insufficiency and activity through suction and pulsion. The empty core is the dynamic that generates activity in self and object components. It is the transcription of biological need into psychic desire. It is the libidinal desire for the object. The erotogenic zones serve as the signifiers of the empty core. It is the driving force of the human personality and of self and object relations. The experience of emptiness also generates ego interests, ambitions, and ideals.

The Uncrossable Void Dividing the Internal and External Object Worlds

In the British psychoanalytic object relations discourse the external and internal object worlds continue to coexist throughout development. The distortions and dissimilarities of the internal world will be greater given the severity of psychopathology, but even in the best of circumstances, these worlds never become completely identical (Fairbairn 1951, Klein 1946). The idea of a void dividing the inner and outer worlds is in accord with contemporary postmodernist philosophy. Derrida (1978) speaks of the void that must inevitably remain between the signifier and signified, and Eco (1984) describes the gap of nothingness that must divide the mental representation from the thing itself that is represented. I suggest that it is the empty core, initially experienced as the lack in instinctual need, that becomes the uncrossable divide between the external and internal object worlds.

Stern (1985) has acknowledged that the British object relations school (Fairbairn 1951, Guntrip 1969, Klein 1946) were unique among clinical theorists in believing that human social relationships were present from birth, suggesting some initial separation between a pristine unitary self and object. Stern therefore questioned Mahler's theory of a symbiotic union between mother and infant preceding separation/

individuation. Stern (1985) suggested that merger fantasies must occur subsequent to separation. The British object relations model of separate internal and external object worlds suggests a resolution for the separation versus symbiosis dilemma. Fairbairn (1941) contends an original separation in the interpersonal relationship between infant and mother. The experience of emptiness and lack result in the internalization of the object relationship and the fantasy of primary identification of self and object. Thus, the internal world of the infant suggests an interesting paradox: the schizoid state of withdrawal is comprised of a phantasy of symbiotic union. Later, it will be seen that this implication of the British object relations theory may be utilized to provide insights into problems such as substance abuse and other addictions to nonhuman objects.

Fairbairn is presenting the theoretical view of contradictory, simultaneously coexisting object relations worlds of separation and symbiosis as different dimensions of experience. In the internal world, there is a primary identification of a symbiotic fusion of self and object followed by gradual separation/individuation. Infantile dependence becomes transitional dependence and finally mature dependence. The implications of the preceding discussion become apparent in a recent discussion with an adult female person. The woman was describing a recent brief visit of a young adult son who was to return abroad to the country where he now lived. Knowledgeable about psychoanalytic views, she alluded to the theories that must be coming to my mind about symbiosis as I listened to her plight. I responded that the anticipated loss was a real one in that her son was not returning to a nearby town but rather going overseas again and that they probably would not see one another for a prolonged period. I said an internal object can only take you so far in substituting for a real one.

Internal objects can make the separation from their external counterparts more tolerable. However, as postmodernist philosophy suggests, a void shall always remain between the mental representation and the thing itself represented. This point speaks to the fact that internal object constancy can never entirely replace the need for the external object world. In fact, when an individual lives completely in his inner world in withdrawal from the external domain it is correct to refer to a schizoid state and not to object constancy. Fairbairn's idea of mature dependence emphasizes that separation/individuation is not predicated upon withdrawal from external object relations.

Similarly to the British object relations dialogue, Lacan (1949), the French psychoanalyst, presented a theory of the schizoid, fragmented infantile self. A dialectical comparison of his viewpoint with that of the British school will further clarify and distinguish the object relations clinical theory of schizoid states.

Jacques Lacan

Lacan (1949) was influenced by Sartre's concept of nothingness (1943) in the psychoanalytic formulation of the importance of "lack" in the development of the infant. Lacan attributed the sense of lack to a "specific prematurity of birth" (p. 4). The infant is born with a gap in his motoric incapacity and advanced perceptual ability. Thus, the sense of lack arises from the fact that the infant cannot sit himself up or manipulate himself as a whole, unitary being, but he can recognize perceptually the boundedness and wholeness of external objects. The infant is viewed as trapped in his motoric incapacity and nursing dependence and experiencing itself as fragmented, disjointed, disjoined. The infant discovers its unitary, specular, bounded, imago in the mirror reflection and identifies with the illusory unitary reflected image that becomes the ideal "I." Henceforth, the infant identifies with the wholeness it perceives in others. Unfortunately, the unitary ideal self remains alienated from the infant's actual fragmented self experience. The striving toward wholeness is perceived as pathological in the sense that the infant endeavors to imagine itself to be what it is not: an ideal, unitary, statuelike, impermeable, impenetrable being.

The Empty Core and Freedom to Shape the Self

There are certain similarities between the views of the British School and Lacan. Both viewpoints stress that the infant is fragmented and striving for wholeness. Furthermore, a sense of lack results in the infant identifying with the object in the imaginary realm. A crucial distinction is that both Klein (1946) and Fairbairn (1951) posit that the infant initially experiences a unitary, pristine sense of self and object. Thus, fragmentation is experienced as a lack in the original sense of wholeness. The emergence of split-off or divided schizoid self states will be experienced in the context of a background ideal of wholeness that is not alienated but derived from an original cohesive state. Therefore, in states of ego splitting and fragmentation, there will always be a counteracting tendency toward synthesis and integration.

Sutherland (1989), who had been a colleague and friend of Fairbairn, stated that if there is a disruption in the child's relationship to the actual parent, there must be a reestablishment of the object connection or the child must have an actual substitute figure. When there is no substitute for the parent, the child creates one imaginatively because the individual cannot shape his own self without an inner image to fill the void, the empty core in which a parental image must be inserted. One might be quickly disposed to the view of an empty core as disadvantageous to the personality. The empty core is in fact central and necessary and has a positive, self-formative value. The child does not only fill the void with an internal image; rather, he plays at comforting, soothing, and mirroring himself in the image of the parental figure. Through this experience the child has the experience of trying out varying modes of the self, parenting himself, and even shaping the self. This idea suggests the existential phenomenological principle that nothingness is the core of freedom, allowing for the individual to shape himself to become what he chooses within the constraints of the given biological and social facticity. Given the emphasis on biological determinism of late, this reminder of a core of human freedom beyond biological contingency is important. As will be shown in a later chapter, the awareness of lack creates desire and ideals. In Sophocles' Theban play, Oedipus of Colonus asks his daughter, Ismene: "When I am nothing/So then I am a man?" (p. 306). Ismene can only respond in the affirmative.

Thus, if the void does not become traumatic or intolerable, it provides the infant with the freedom of nothingness to practice at shaping himself in the imago of the object. The empty core gives rise to the grandiose self (Kohut 1977), which results in realistic ambitions and ego interests. I believe that this void would be created by the child himself in his own spontaneous striving toward autonomy if external circumstances did not create the void through disruptions. If the disruptions become traumatic or prolonged, the internal object world becomes disappointing because it is basically insubstantial and unreal. The empty core may become the bottomless pit of the schizoid patient. He generally adopts one of two strategies to deal with the empty core. The first is the effort to eliminate all need by maintaining himself as aloof, self-sufficient, isolated. Emptiness becomes an ideal. The individual strives toward extinguishing all need. The second strategy is the endeavor to arrive at a stage of absolute completion, fullness, fulfillment. It too is an endeavor to extinguish need, but through satiation.

MICHAEL BALINT AND THE BASIC FAULT

Balint's theory of the "basic fault" is comparable to Fairbairn's views on pathological emptiness and serves to further explicate the psychodynamics of the schizoid condition. Balint (1968) states that the infant is in need of primary love from the caregiver for its emotional well-being just as it requires oxygen for biological survival. The primary love relationship is comprised of holding, mirroring, and responsive attunement. Winnicott described two aspects of the mother's relationship to the infant distinguishing the environmental mother, who provides active ego care, from the part-object mother, who is a passive target of the infant's instinctual need. Thus the environmental mother provides ego care through her primary love of the infant.

Balint states that there may be a failure in primary love in the earliest formative phase either as a result of congenital deficiencies on the part of the infant to extract from the environment or as a result of insufficiency of support, attention, or holding on the part of the caregiver. The failure in primary love gives rise to the basic fault, which is experienced by the infant as a state of lack, emptiness, and deadness. Balint emphasizes that the term basic fault refers to an irregularity or defect in overall psychic structure. This deficiency becomes manifested in oral greed and addictive states.

In ordinary development, the libidinal oral relationship to the part-object serves as a channel for the infant to find the whole environmental mother of ego care. When there is a failure in primary love, the infant loses hope of finding the environmental whole object and the instinctual need for the exciting part-object serves to entirely replace and compensate for the need for ego care.

THE SCHIZOID INCAPACITY TO TOLERATE THE SUBJECTIVE FREEDOM OF THE HUMAN OTHER

Unable to tolerate the inability to control human relationships, the schizoid often transfers his libidinal investment to nonhuman things. What is at issue is that the other individual in a relationship is free to reject him. Given his extreme sensitivity to rejection, the schizoid person cannot tolerate the subjective freedom of the other. If the schizoid becomes involved in a human relationship, he may attempt to transform the other into a thinglike object.

The following brief case example illustrates this theory. Thomas was a middle-aged patient who was habitually autocratic in his relationships. He lived with his lover, Ann. I occasionally met with them conjointly and therefore directly witnessed their interaction. Ann had considerably less education, sophistication, and worldly experience than Thomas. He saw himself molding Ann into his idea of the ideal woman and conceived of her as his creation. He selected her clothing and dictated how she should dress. He introduced her to the theater, art, music, literature, and fine restaurants. He insisted that her taste in these areas should be identical to his own. Gradually, Ann grew more confident and expressed opinions and preferences herself. She was surprised when Thomas, who had always been kind and supportive, devalued her interests as tasteless and reflective of her poor education. He became jealous, complaining that she responded to gestures of friendship from persons outside of his influence. He wanted

Ann's life to revolve exclusively around him and she increasingly complained that he treated her as a possession or a doll and did not allow her to have a life of her own. Buber (1958) distinguished two types of object relations in his philosophical designations of the I–thou and the I–it relationships. Buber suggested that the I–thou situation is one of two subjectivities while the I–it relationship refers to a subject and thinglike object. Laing (1959) protested that the term object dehumanized the other as a person by objectifying him into a thing. Laing objected to the mechanistic language of psychoanalysis. Laing's criticism did not take into account the mechanistic aspects of the human psyche. The internalization of a relationship is an endeavor to transform a threatening subjective other into an object. Thus, the internalization of an object is a form of psychic alchemy in terms of the subjective external other being transformed into a thinglike object. Only through the developmental process does the thinglike part object become transformed into a fully human, free subject.

The schizoid's endeavor to achieve a state of absolute omnipotent fulfillment of the empty core is enacted in the compulsive need for thinglike nonhuman objects. The compulsive urge toward drugs, alcohol, food, money, clothing, and sexual conquests may all serve in the effort to fill the void with nonhuman objects. In the case of the non-schizoid person, the interest in the thing-world adaptively serves the autonomous self in separating from the human world. The empty core of the schizoid patient is bottomless and cannot be filled.

The instinctual need for the part-object only creates greater need. The individual becomes consumed with his greed and may therefore strive for a state of absolute emptiness and the extinction of need. The anorexic eating disorder may reflect the schizoid ideal of emptiness. The hungry body becomes a metaphor for the empty psychic core. Kafka's short story, "The Hunger Artist" illustrates the ideal of emptiness. The hunger artist is a circus player who starves himself of food for a prolonged period before a large audience. As he wastes away, the audience grows in number. Only when he is near death, does the audience dwindle.

THE VAMPIRISH EMPTY SELF OF THE SCHIZOID PERSONALITY

The schizoid individual is starving for love. This hungry self is radically repressed. The repressed self's hunger is an emptiness longing for fulfillment. The hunger for love may be transformed into a need for sex, food, money, beliefs, anything imaginable. The greed for the thing-world also threatens to consume the patient so that it too is repressed.

Guntrip (1969) stated that the schizoid patient may appear aloof and isolated from interpersonal relationships in order to defend himself against an all-consuming need to be loved. Kohut (1971) said that the schizoid individual may be conscious of a longing for intimacy but repudiates it because of the fear of rejection.

A young adult female patient, Lisa, was a college student who experienced a pattern of all-consuming, destructive, romantic relationships typically followed by intervals of isolation, detachment, and indifference to relationships. Lisa's romantic relationships were all-consuming in the sense that after only a few weeks of meeting her lover, she felt as if she could not live without him and that her well-being depended upon their relationship. She craved his presence and could not tolerate any separations. When the lover would want to go home at the end of an evening, she would plead with him to stay and if he insisted upon departing, she became desperate and even threatened to take her own life.

Superficially, Lisa resembled the classic borderline patient in that she could not concentrate upon her schoolwork or any of her own individuated activities but completely lost herself in the symbiotic union with the love object. Masterson (1976) described the classic borderline patient as seeking symbiotic union to avoid the abandonment depression and separation anxiety associated with individuation. Lisa's need to cling to the symbiotic union was experienced with the desperation of a life-and-death situation. She felt that she needed the object for her well-being as desperately as one needs oxygen for biological survival. Balint (1968) emphasizes that the schizoid patient suffering from the basic fault longs for romantic love or manifests addictions not basically as an expression of conflict and defense, but rather as a futile effort to receive the primary love needed to shore up a deficient psychic structure.

Another factor in Lisa's romantic relationships that suggested their schizoid quality was the primarily subjective nature of the object. Winnicott's views on the subjective and the objective object will clarify this idea.

WINNICOTT, THE SUBJECTIVE OBJECT, AND THE SCHIZOID PATIENT

Winnicott described the schizoid patient as primarily related to a subjective (exciting) object. In ordinary development, the infant experiences the illusion of creating the libidinal object that meets instinctual and ego needs. This process is referred to as the relationship to the subjective object. The subjective object is experienced as not only created by the infant but existing only to meet the infant's needs. The subjective object enables the infant to tolerate the separation between self and object and not become overwhelmed by separation anxiety. For the infant to preserve the illusion of the subjective object for an optimal period, the actual caregiver must, for a limited time, be so empathically attuned to the baby's needs that it is permitted the illusion that the object is an extension of the self.

Lisa often stated that she endeavored to create the perfect boyfriend. Psychodynamically, her statement may be translated into meaning that she endeavored to create a subjective object. The basically subjective nature of her object relations was evident in the identical characteristics of each of her relationships regardless of the differences in the actual external objects. In other words, Lisa fell in love in exactly the same way as if it were the same person again and again. In fact, one boyfriend expressed surprise at her exclamations of love and suggested that she could not possibly love him for who he was since she hardly knew him.

Fairbairn (1944) described three stages in the development of object relations. The first is that of infantile dependence characterized by what Winnicott designated as the primary subjective nature of the object. The schizoid patient struggles primarily with the need to create and maintain the subjective object. The concept of the subjective object is comparable to the idea of the symbiotic object in American ego psychology. The second stage is referred to as the intermediate stage of transition characterized by an internal object that has a combination of both subjective and objective features. The transitional internal object is comprised of the actual attributes of the parental object and the child's fantasies and distortions about those figures. I have described how the borderline patient is typically dominated by such internal objects (1990). In the transitional intermediate phase, the child struggles to differentiate itself from the internal object (Fairbairn 1944). Thus, Mahler and colleagues' (1975) subphases of separation/individuation are identical to this intermediate phase of differentiation in which the subjective object gradually is transformed into the objective object. The third and final stage, mature dependence, is comprised of the achieve-

ment of the objective object characterized by the child's recognition that the object has motivations, interests, and a life of
its own separate from those of the child, and the child develops the capacity for concern for the object's own sake. This
stage is identical with that of the achievement of object constancy in American ego psychology.

In the British school of object relations, the subjective
object is not entirely lost as the objective object gains ascend-
ence. Winnicott states that the subjective object continues to
have a psychic place in the potential, transitional area (not to
be confused with Fairbairn's intermediate, transitional stage
described above) of creativity, illusion, and play.

THE DESTRUCTION OF THE SUBJECTIVE OBJECT IN SCHIZOID STATES

Winnicott states that in ordinary development, the infant's
libidinal gratification of desire temporarily annihilates the
object. In his terms, the infant's gratification of a good feed
destroys the object. This suggestive idea may be translated to
mean that the subjective object is primarily a need–gratifying
object and therefore, when the infant's satisfaction results in
its no longer needing the object, the object thereby ceases to
exist in the infant's mind and is therefore annihilated. Winnicott is posing the important suggestion that for the infant, the
object only exists in a state of desire; libidinal gratification is
associated with object loss and the threat of an objectless state.
The patient, Lisa, oscillated between periods of intense object
need and intervals of complete isolation and disinterest in
objects. Lisa stated that when a boy treated her well or acqui-
esced to her demands, she was not easily satisfied but became
needier. She would feel insatiable and make more demands.
She was aware of a vague sense that if she allowed herself to

feel satisfied or secure in the boyfriend's caring for her, she would lose all interest and forget about him. This anxiety became apparent in an intense and stormy relationship in which she and a boyfriend spent every day together fighting and making up. When she finally became interested in pursuing some minimal activities for herself that would not include the boyfriend she was seized with a panic attack. She explored this problem and became aware that she was not afraid that the boyfriend would desert her for her individuation but rather that if she ceased to think of him and involved herself in a new interest, she might forget about him altogether. At this point she could see that the obsessional quality of her love relationships was related to a fear of object loss. The borderline patient does not primarily fear that the gratification of libidinal need will destroy the subjective object but rather that his efforts to aggressively differentiate from the internal object at the stage of transition will result in the destruction of the object.

Most caregivers responsible for an ordinary infant sometimes feel emptied, worn out, and communicate, "What is it you want, my blood?" Therefore, the infant may fleetingly discover itself in the caregiver's response as greedy and vampirish. In the case of the nonschizoid patient, the parent is replenished, revitalized, and returns in a plenitude of being. The infant is reassured that he has not drained the parent beyond recovery. Thus, its sense of itself as a vampire is mitigated and only excess need is repressed. In this way, the infant gradually recognizes that the object exists between feeds, giving rise to the transformation of the subjective object into the objective object.

In the case of the schizoid patient, there is no such rapprochement. The caregiver is experienced as remaining worn out, emptied, and injured. In Lisa's case, the mother had been emotionally immature, physically ill, and overwhelmed by a difficult environment in Lisa's first year of life. She was caught between an all-consuming need for primary love and the fear that libidinal need and satisfaction would empty and destroy the object.

It is the intensity of schizoid hunger that accounts for the patient's efforts to repress it and go through life as an automaton. In repression, the isolated, hungry self can only become hungrier, emptier. Hunger is no longer a need but transformed into an identity component. He ceases to be a baby calling out because he is hungry. The cry is silenced. Hunger is no longer a need and a cry but rather a state of mind.

MULTIPLICITY OF SUB-SELF SYSTEMS

Sutherland (1989) has advanced Fairbairn's work on schizoid states, suggesting that the splitting of the self refers to highly complex organizations of the personality, each functioning as a separate individual expressing a need for a relationship with another person. Fairbairn (1944) has described ego segments as dynamic structures related to internal objects. Sutherland states that the ego segments are sub-self systems and that each sub-self is a dynamic personification and whole in itself.

The primary desire is for a relationship with the parental figure. Failures in the relationship result in a void that the individual attempts to fill by the creating of imaginary relationships. These are constituted by two sub-selves, each related to internal objects in the imaginary realm. There is a sub-self of frustrated need for optimal contact with the caregiver. The sense of emptiness is expressed as the need for an exciting (but nongratifying) internal object. There is another sub-self that is identified with the rejecting response of the caregiver to the self for having such needs. The two sub-selves have a powerful dynamic relationship with one another. The anti-relational self identified with the caregiver's rejecting attitude is permanently at war with the unacceptable relational needs. It aggressively attacks both the infantile relational self and the forbidden exciting object. The internal objects are described as dynamic images of persons with human qualities: exciting and rejecting objects.

Fairbairn does not reject drive theory but rather places libido and aggression in the service of object relations. The libido serves object connection; aggression serves separation. Aggression is secondary to libido (but a drive potential in its own right) and works in the service of the repression of libido. The war between the internal sub-selves permits the central self to seek an ideal adaptation to the external object world void of overly exciting or rejecting aspects (Sutherland 1989).

The two sub-selves are presented as consequences of frustrated needs. I propose that the dynamic activity of each sub-self is based upon an empty core of need. Fairbairn views the internal sub-selves in a state of permanent warfare. This situation would foreclose the possibility of conflict resolution. I suggest that aspects of the anti-relational self may become an autonomous self. This proposal implies that there may be autonomous states that are not just defensive against relational needs. According to Storr (1988) solitude can be an important state in its own right, especially in relationship to the creative process. Object relations theory needs to take into account a striving for solitude and autonomy that is not defensively anti-relational. Its anti-relational manifestation reflects either primitive development or a psychopathological state.

A clinical vignette will illustrate how the multiplicity of sub-selves is manifested (or disguised) in the patient's clinical narrative.

The client, Bruce, was a young adult male. Successful in his professional life as a corporate attorney he came for treatment because of difficulties in establishing meaningful personal relationships. In one session, he said he thought of discussing his parents' families but wondered if this were appropriate. It seemed unrelated and he feared he would ramble. He was told to discuss whatever he wanted however he felt like it. It will be seen that schizoid patients often describe their current inner object worlds as they discuss other persons in the outer object world.

Bruce first recalled a dream of long ago. He dreamed that he had awakened from a bad dream, descended the stairs, and woke up. His association to the dream within a dream was that the dream occurred too long ago to have significance. Then he added that if somebody else told him the dream, he would think: the dreamer was lonely. There was a bad dream and he awakened and no one was there. Bruce then recalled that if he were descending the stairs, he would be seen by his parents in the living room. However, in the dream, there was no thought of them. He concluded that their absence was significant. They would have been watching him. Maybe the dream was a wish to be seen, recognized.

In Bruce's dream, we see the divided self in the two dreamers. Bruce dreaming of a dreamer. Secondly, his remark "if someone told me this dream" also reflects a divided self. He can only discuss the meaning of the dream from the point of view of another—the somebody is a dissociated self state.

Bruce continued to discuss his parents' families. He announced that he is the only family member without a brother. He had a sister. His sister had him as a brother, and both of his parents had brothers. He discussed his mother's relationship to her brothers. Of most significance is her relationship to a brother whom she unrealistically idealizes though he is an ordinary, unimpressive individual. The therapist wondered why Bruce thinks she needs to idealize the brother. As Bruce discussed the brother, he made an unconscious slip, referring to him as "my brother" instead of his mother's brother. He noticed this slip but then went on to discuss his mother's poor relationship to her own father who never was someone she could look up to. Her idealization of the brother reflected the wish to have a good object relationship to the parental figure.

Bruce's unconscious slip is suggestive of an identification

with his mother. He also has a poor relationship with the father. In calling his uncle his brother he is revealing an identification with the mother in the need for a good father. Here the mother does not represent a parental image but an infantile dependent self. She may also represent his female self longing to have a tie to his father. Bruce's sister is close to the father. Ultimately, the dream may reflect Bruce's wish to be his sister so that father would love him and he would not have to compete with him in an oedipal situation. The transference bears out this interpretation. At the end of the session, Bruce continued to talk, did not acknowledge the time was complete and did not want to leave. Thus the wish to be loved by the father is unconsciously activated in the transference and described through the displacement of the narrative concerning his parents' relatives.

This vignette illustrates how divided sub-selves of the personality seek relationships with parental images. Based upon disappointing external object relations, the self is not a static entity nor a mere representation, but rather a dynamic, active, structural sub-self system. Fairbairn views the personality as unconsciously based upon multiple dynamic sub-self systems expressing a need for relationships with internal object images based on external counterparts.

2

CAPTURED IN THE REFLECTION OF THE MIRROR

It will be shown that in the schizoid position, the infant seeks communication and mirroring from the outer, object world but also fears impingement, loss of self to object, and the dread of being captured in the reflection of the mirroring other. An object relations understanding of the schizoid stage points toward the positive and adaptive aspects of this developmental position.

MELANIE KLEIN

Klein (1946) took a pioneering step forward in structuring internal objects into the infant right from the start. Klein was among the first of analysts to use the play technique in the treatment of children (1926); she brought the infant's relationship to the mother to the fore of personality development and she discovered the infant's destructive, violent phantasies and primitive defenses against the ensuing psychotic anxieties.

29

Klein (1946) remarked upon the ubiquity of the infant's destructive oral greed and envy, which she based upon oral sadism derived from the biological force of Freud's death instinct. According to Klein, the infant projectively identified the life and death instincts into the maternal breast resulting in the split-off libidinal good breast and aggressive bad breast. The death instinct threatened the infant with self-annihilation if it was not projectively identified into the breast, which transformed it into aggression. Once the infant perceived the bad breast (and not itself) as the source of aggression, it could direct any surplus aggression toward the bad breast in self-defense. Klein (1946) referred to this primary development stage as the paranoid-schizoid position.

For the infant at around 6 months of age, advances in cognitive development and the fusion of libido and aggression resulted in the mother no longer being split into good and bad part-objects; she became known as a whole person. Once it was recognized that the mother could be both good and bad, the infant entered into the depressive position. The phantasy of the injured mother could be overcome through compensatory efforts of love and reparation (Klein 1935).

W. R. D. FAIRBAIRN

Fairbairn (1940, 1941, 1944) accepted Klein's internal object world but not the concept that it is derived primarily from the biological forces of Freud's life and death instincts. Fairbairn conceived the human as a social animal and conceptualized the internal object world primarily on a social and not a biological basis. He emphasized that the infant must develop the capacity to live in mature dependence among others, that is, recognizing their "otherness" while engaged in survival tasks (Sutherland 1989). He believed that the innate characteristics of humans must be mediated through the family group. He suggests that although the infant originally relates through the taking in of the object world through the means of incorporation, there is a shift whereby giving to others emotionally becomes more dominant than taking (1940).

For Fairbairn, orality refers not only to the need for pleasure and milk but to a hunger for personal loving contact. If love is lacking, the infant is aware of something missing and responds through the intensification of oral incorporative need (Sutherland 1989). Spitz's research studies (1965) provide ample evidence for Fairbairn's theory by demonstrating that the absence of the caregiver's personal involvement in the care of the infant results in the loss of the spirited striving to grow, to explore, and ultimately even to live.

Fairbairn's contention that the infant has a sense of the caregiver as a whole person and not merely as a breast refers to the need for personal, loving contact. Fairbairn's work has not become widely accepted by American psychoanalysts partly because he is sometimes read too literally. The infant initially perceives the mother as a whole object. This is not a sophisticated, cognitive understanding on the part of the infant but rather a vague, primarily affective sense of the object's wholeness and subjectivity.

Fairbairn (1941) agrees with Klein about the importance of the breast as a part object but differs with her concerning its origin. Klein (1946) conceives of the part-object as an a priori aspect of the instinctual drive. It is only subsequent to prolonged and dependable experience that the infant knows the object as a whole person. Fairbairn contends that the infant has a sense of the whole person from the start and it is only through failures in personal object relating that the infant relates solely to the breast. There is a disintegration of object relations whereby the infant compensates through purely need-gratifying, part-object relating, and autoeroticism.

Spitz's studies (1965) provide support for this view by demonstrating that infants deprived of personal involvement with their caregivers desperately resort to need-satisfying autoeroticism.

In Fairbairn's theory, autoeroticism is symbolically expressive of the relationship to the internal part-object; for instance, the thumb is conceived as a substitute for the internal breast. Failures in external object relating result in the depersonalization of the object world. The infant loses its sense of the whole mother and instead relates to her desperately as a pure "it," a mere object without sensitivity. However, I must now qualify my previous comments in that in the depersonalization of the object world, internal object relations remain based upon significant familial relationships. Part-objects are deteriorated or degraded substitutes for whole persons (Sutherland 1989) but still retain their human, personal characteristics. Self object functions are only internalized in the image of a person. This personal factor is a distinguishing feature of Fairbairn's object relations theory.

Fairbairn does not reject Klein's emphasis on greed, envy, and sadism but bases their origins on destructive personal experience and not a biological death drive. He also places the advent of aggression later than Klein. He describes the schizoid position as pre-ambivalent and associates aggression with the depressive position and the acquisition of teeth. Sutherland (1989) makes the important point that whether or not one believes in the death instinct, there can be little doubt that the infant manifests negative, rejective reactions such as screaming, spitting, and pushing away before the acquisition of biting. I will expand upon these remarks throughout the remaining sections of this chapter to describe a paranoid aspect to the schizoid position from a purely object relational point of view. The object relations perspective does not imply an abandonment of drive theory but views libido and aggression as serving object connection or separation.

DISCOVERING ONE'S REFLECTION
IN THE LOOK OF THE OTHER

The emptiness of the schizoid core spurs the individual toward acquiring a sense of himself as real by the recognition of the other (Hegel 1807, Kohut 1971, Lacan 1949, Sartre 1943, Winnicott 1971). The infant originally turns to the mother for mirroring to acquire a witness to the reality of its being. The infant discovers its nature reflected in the response of the caregiver. Sartre (1943) originally referred to the infant finding itself reflected in the caregiver's look but he was not referring simply to the eye of the caregiver but rather to its total response to the infant. Being recognized by the other may give rise to either pride or shame. Fairbairn's view that the infant internalizes the object in order to control it says nothing about how the infant operationalizes this strategy. The French have always been generally more attuned to the subtle arts of seduction. Thus Lacan (1988) and Sartre (1943) speak of the infant's desire to become the object of the caregiver's desire. It is in the intricacies of the libidinal self's seduction of the exciting object that we see the balance between the self's wish to transform the object entirely into a thinglike "it" and the need to preserve its free subjectivity.

The libidinal self endeavors to win over the exciting object by making itself admirable, exciting, an irresistible object of desire. Yet the libidinal self does not want the exciting object to be forced into slavery but rather to freely choose the libidinal self as the object of desire. In other words, the libidinal self endeavors to become the object of desire to the exciting object and thereby transform it into a love slave. However, the libidinal self wants the exciting object to freely choose its position as love slave revealing the underlying need to be loved that spurs on the erotic seduction. This also reveals how libidinal desire serves the individual's need to be loved in the internal object world. The pattern of internalized object relating described above is often acted out in interpersonal relations as the ensuing chapters will describe. In seeking to make itself the object of the other's desire, the libidinal self is desperately threatened by the mother desiring anything other than the infant. Thus the caregiver's subjective desires outside of the infant threaten it with separation and is at the root of jealousy. Eventually, this situation results in the Oedipus triangular situation.

In endeavoring to become the object of the other's desire, the infant is threatened with the loss of its own subjectivity, with the possibility that it will be no more but a mere object to the other. I refer to this dilemma as the infant's anxiety that it will be captured in the reflection of the mirroring object. This is what I consider the paranoid component of the schizoid position. It gives rise to a wish to disappear and become invisible. Games of peek-a-boo and hide-and-seek have been understood in ego psychological terms as an endeavor to master separation anxiety. They also are reflective of the infant's wish to disappear and escape, becoming petrified into the object of the other's subjectivity. The escape effort is powered by the infant's aggression manifested by the rejective reactions described (Sutherland 1989).

These issues refer to the internal object world. There is initially an effort to transform a relationship between subjectivities to one in which the object becomes an "it" or a thing. In order to achieve this, the libidinal self endeavors to seduce the exciting object by becoming the object of the other's desire. The libidinal self now perceives itself as an object. This possibility is laid out by the infant who initially discovers itself reflected in the look of the caregiver. The implication is that the infant discovers itself in its otherness (in how it is perceived by the other). It is the object's view of the infant as other that the infant internalizes. Speaking in classical psychoanalytic terms, Fairbairn describes a primary identification between the infant and mother in the internal object world. The infant struggles to differentiate from this identification. I am translating Fairbairn's view to mean that in order to recognize the reality of his existence in the only way he can, the infant identifies his subjectivity with the object's viewpoint in order to perceive himself as he is recognized by others. Thus, the infant's first sense of self is that of an object. His subjectivity is projectively identified into the other as he begins to see himself from other points of view. He discovers himself in his otherness to the object.

THE SELF CAPTURED IN THE REFLECTION OF THE LOOK OF THE OTHER

The infant experiences a beginning sense of alienation from the sense of self since he must discover it in the look of the other and its "otherness" to another. He attempts to turn the tables by becoming the object of desire to the other and thereby using the sense of self as object to his own advantage. This libidinal, erotic strategy of infantile sexuality may be understood as the first manifestation of subjectivity. The child endeavors to transform the other into an it or a thing, a libidinalized, exciting part-object, but the need for love and personal involvement becomes manifest in the wish that the other freely accept the role of love slave or part-object. The mode of being the self as object finds expression throughout life in the universal tendencies persons have to fantasize about themselves in many situations from the vantage position of an imagined observer, perceiving themselves from the outside, from the point of view of someone not identified as one's subjective I. In such instances, subjectivity is projected into the other while the self is seen exclusively as an object.

ILLUSTRATIONS
OF THE PARANOID ASPECTS
OF THE SCHIZOID POSITION

The paranoid aspect of the schizoid position is often a pronounced feature in schizoid patients. Primitive belief systems such as voodoo, witchcraft, or the fear of being photographed reflect this paranoid aspect. The idea that the witch doctor may harm a person by injuring a relic or possession of the would-be victim, or destroying or sticking pins into a material likeness or image of the individual, is entirely comparable to the paranoid anxiety about being an object to another's subjectivity.

A female adult patient was isolated. In her fantasy life she had a series of intense love affairs with persons whom she barely knew. She experienced these love affairs daily, similar to a soap opera. In her most recent fantasied love affairs, she was infatuated with her English teacher. One day several weeks after the course had been completed, she unexpectedly met him. He astounded her by saying he had thought and dreamed of her. She was in a panic. What became apparent in the course of the analysis was that her terror was not due to the temptation of a forbidden, symbolically incestuous affair, but rather more basically, that she was the object of another person's thoughts or dreams. The idea that he thought negatively or positively about her threatened her with becoming whatever he thought of her. She felt that if she became involved with him she would be consumed with endless worries about how he perceived her. She had avoided all relationships because she feared becoming petrified into the object of the other. She restricted her relationships to the world of fantasy to assure that she could remain the subject in control of the other as object.

THE TRUE SELF MEDIATED
THROUGH OBJECT RELATIONS

The infant must discover its nature through the mediation of the other. Even the research studies on temperament are necessarily subjective. Chess describes three general types of temperament: (1) the easy child, (2) the difficult child, (3) the slow-to-warm-up child. The study categorizes the infant in terms of rhythmicity of biological needs, adaptability to change, fretfulness, easiness. The descriptions of the temperaments actually refer to the response of the caregiver or object—how the object finds the infant to be slow, easy, difficult. In other words, one cannot get away from subjective viewpoint because the infant is easy or difficult for another person. The description of the infant's temperamental nature must be within the context of a relationship. Likewise, the infant discovers his temperament through the response of the other, which is also based upon the other's temperament, frustration tolerance, anxiety tolerance, and so on.

In existential phenomenological terms, the infant discovers its true self, which includes biological temperament, cognitive capacity, appearance, through the response of the other. The infant therefore discovers itself in the mode-of-being for others (Sartre 1943). The conception of being-for-others is analogous to the Kleinian idea of the infant becoming incorporated by the other and gives rise to comparable anxieties. In being for the other, the infant becomes aware of a lack of being-for-itself. It sees itself in its otherness, as object to the other's subjectivity and endeavors to wrest back its subjectivity by the desire to flee from the sight of the other. To become invisible, to be unseen, is to annihilate one's reflection in the eye of the other. This is the origin of the need for solitude and privacy, to make oneself into something more than what others perceive one to be. Thus the needs for recognition and solitude dialectically coexist in the realm of the internal world. The negativistic, rejective tendencies described by Sutherland (1989) are the behavioral manifestation of this need to turn away, to become invisible, to escape being in the sight of the other.

In his seminal paper of 1971, "Mirror Role of Mother and Family in Child Development," Winnicott says:

> What does the infant see when he or she looks into the mother's face? I am suggesting that ordinarily, what the infant sees is himself or herself. In other words, the mother is looking at the baby and what she looks like is related to what she sees there. [p. 112]

It is imperative for the infant to find himself, his own true nature, reflected in the mother's look and not her own troubled mood, her own image of who he should be instead of who he is or worse yet, no sign of him at all. The caregiver provides supportive mirroring by responding to the infant's gestures rather than by imposing her own gestures and cues and forcing the infant to respond to them. The caregiver also responds by recognizing the child's gesture but not stealing it for herself.

Therapists struggle with identical issues. A schizoid child randomly dropped materials on my floor. I quietly observed her. The child began to form the droppings into a pattern. I simply commented "a pattern." The child immediately destroyed the emerging order. My comment was precipitous in that the child had not yet fully claimed the pattern as her own. The remark stole from her the pattern of her emerging sense of self by subtly claiming credit for her structuring of experience. Rather than surrender her pattern, the child destroyed it. Optimal mirroring would have been just being there showing interest in her and the activity.

There will be occasions when the patient rejects more supportive modes of mirroring. The patient individuates in the paranoid-schizoid position by annihilating his image in the therapist's look. The patient's negativistic, rejecting reactions are a part of the process and, similarly to the caregiver, the therapist supports the development of the patient's self by allowing him to annihilate the therapist's vision of him. The therapist must allow the patient to get out of the range of his empathy, understanding, and interpretations. No doubt, empathic understanding is the most important ingredient in the treatment of the schizoid individual. At the same time, the therapist must not idealize empathy. For the schizoid patient, empathy can be as ensnaring and objectifying as any other intervention, even more so because, like pure honey, it tempts the patient into its sticky, thick warmth.

FAIRBAIRN AND EGO AND SELF PSYCHOLOGIES

The patient seeking and rejecting recognition enters into what Fairbairn describes as the transitional stage between infantile dependence and mature dependence. This stage is analogous to Mahler's separation/individuation (1975). In a previous work (Seinfeld 1990) I stated that the ego psychological object relations dialogue has emphasized the dangers of symbiosis to autonomy. I took exception arguing for the positive value of symbiosis for autonomy. I would now add that I believe the infant has a pristine but unitary autonomous self that is never entirely lost in the close bond to the mother. The attachment serves to reflect and enhance the autonomous self, not to threaten it. As Sutherland (1989) aptly states, the development of the autonomous self may be likened to an acorn becoming a tree. The close bond between the infant and mother does not in itself impede the infant from becoming what his nature intends. Mahler (1975) recognizes this fact when she refers to an autonomous drive. Symbiosis remains a useful term if it is not defined in a biological state of absolute fusion. It refers to an affective state of oneness, a phantasy of alikeness that Fairbairn described in classical terms as primary identification. It remains an autonomous self—no matter how pristine—that phantasizes or feels such alikeness with the internal object.

The transitional stage is marked by a separation from the internal object, which therefore gives rise to separation anxiety, isolation, and fears of object loss, prompting the wish to return again to the object. Clinging to the mother may be affectively felt as a merged state in terms of the wish to deny separation. However, clinging to the object creates the fear of the loss of autonomy thus setting in motion the recurrence of the cycle. Optimally, each cycle of closeness–distance gives rise to growth toward mature dependence. Fairbairn's transitional stage is comparable to Mahler's rapprochement stage. Jacobson's views (1964) that the drives are shaped by an active self in an external, social, object world is quite similar to Fairbairn's views and advance ego psychology to a complete object relations theory.

Heinz Kohut has seemingly advanced an object relations view in focusing on the development of the self in relation to objects. However, the goals of the self, ideals, and ambitions, are entirely individualistic. As Chodorow (1989) points out about Kohut's views: "In his version, the object relations route is to lead to individual fulfillment of individual goals" (p. 254). Therefore, although there are many similarities in the ideas of Fairbairn and Kohut (Seinfeld 1990), these views on the outcome of development differ entirely.

Fairbairn is one of the few analysts who has viewed the outcome of development in terms of mature dependence upon a community of relationships in which otherness and separateness are acknowledged while persons share in survival and living tasks. His views do not neglect the importance of individuation but rather emphasize that the individual arrives at independence with a built-in social sense. He explicitly states that in mature dependence an attitude of emotionally giving is dominant over the earlier attitude of taking. Fairbairn also emphasizes the family as the primary social group in sharing socialization, survival, and living tasks. The positive aspects of schizoid phenomena are often overlooked.

THE EMPTY CORE AND THE HUNGER OF IMAGINATION

The infant withdraws into the psychic interior from discontent in external object relations. Fairbairn (1944) believed that a satisfied infant would have no need to internalize the object. This view overlooks the adaptive, creative aspects of internalization and the development of psychic structure.

Hartmann (1950) expresses the view that the individual may first turn inward out of frustration but later because he has come to know the adaptive advantages of internalization. The individual takes a detour inward and exercises ego functions as a rehearsal for acting upon the external world. Hartmann also has a sense that the internal world must be personalized in his theory that object constancy is the central ego function around which the other ego functions develop. Fairbairn (1944) believes that the internal object world is the realm of the imaginary and comprises the personality structure. Therefore, the implication of his own views is that the internal object world is necessary for creative adaptation. As Storr (1988) states: "If man, like some insects, was preprogrammed to be more or less perfectly adapted to this environment, he would live a stereotyped life with neither the need to look for anything better nor the capacity to imagine it" (p. viii). Storr argues that a degree of discontentment that is not traumatically overwhelming fosters creative adaptation and achievement. Thus, Storr (1988) states "man's creative adaptability paradoxically derives from his primary lack of adaptation" (p. viii). It is this sense of primary lack that I have described as the empty core or the experience of existential nothingness.

WINNICOTT, THE SECRET, NONCOMMUNICATING SELF, AND SEPARATION AND SOLITUDE

Winnicott (1963) states "Although healthy persons communicate and enjoy communicating, the other fact is equally true, that *each individual is an isolate, permanently non-communicating, permanently unknown, in fact unfound*" (p. 187). Winnicott is referring to an aspect of the self that needs to remain private, protected from impingement of the external world and out of communication with external reality. This viewpoint suggests that internalization may not only be the result of environmental failure, but rather that the infant may have its own motivation for adaptive self-initiated internalization. In such instances, the isolated, private self may capitalize on optimal, nontraumatic experiences of discontent, in order to effect the internalization process. The infant's need to be mirrored refers to its healthy need to communicate and enjoy communicating with the external object world. The infant's efforts to escape from being captured in the mirroring reflection of the object is reflective of its need to preserve the privacy and solitude of the core, true self. Winnicott states, "At the center of each person is an incommunicado element, and this is sacred and most worthy of preservation" (p. 187). Thus, Winnicott suggests that the ordinary primitive defenses and the paranoid aspects of the schizoid position are in the service of protecting the core, private self.

These views of Winnicott suggest that the infant may be inclined to internalize a good object not only in secondary defense against bad objects but also to support the inner secret, isolated self in its efforts to remain withdrawn from the external object world. I understand the separation/individuation process and associated object constancy described by Mahler (1975) to be initially motivated by the secret self's need for privacy and an internal good object to lessen excessive need for external objects.

Many of the chapters to follow illustrate pathological schizoid states. The brief clinical vignettes to follow will illustrate how creative and adaptive achievements may also arise from schizoid states.

Arthur was a 16-year-old Afro-American youngster. He grew up in a chaotic, homeless family comprised of his mother, maternal grandmother, and a host of aunts and cousins who were regularly on the family scene. Arthur's mother was heroin-addicted and his grandmother was depressed and ill with heart disease. Arthur never knew his father, whose whereabouts were unknown. The family had lived in city shelters and in welfare hotels.

Arthur was a gifted and creative youngster. Throughout his childhood he was an avid reader and described his books as an escape from the difficult world around him. He also coped by transforming his life circumstances into imaginative play. One apartment where they lived had been completely infested by cockroaches. Arthur would sit all day upon the floor with cardboard and rocks he had collected in the street. He created stories about the cockroaches being criminals. He would apprehend a couple of roaches and imprison them beneath cardboard covered by a rock. Eventually, he might release the roaches for good behavior. He would play such games for hours on end; the adults would always note how well he could entertain himself. In this way, Arthur experienced a sense of power or control in his life. He would make up stories and play for hours on end that he was the all-conquering general or king vanquishing his foes and protecting his poor soldiers or subjects. In the family, he assumed a parental function. He did all the family shopping, laundering, and cleaning. As a latency child, he would wheel his cart full of the family laundry to the neighborhood laundromat every Sunday to the admiration of the adult neighbors, who would remark on what a good, responsible youngster he was. The adults in his family were often overwhelmed by ordinary demands or expectations on their own lives. If his mother had to attend a Fair Hearing at the Welfare Board, Arthur would accompany her and miss school to insure that she kept her appointment. If his grandmother was ill, he would accompany her to the physician. During his free time, he was always stopping into the local stores to see if there was work he could do to earn money. He would then give almost his entire earnings to his family.

In return for the responsibilities he shouldered, Arthur was given complete freedom. The adults never told him what to do nor did they treat him as a child. In early adolescence, he could stay out at night as late as he wished. On occasion, he encountered difficulties at school if a teacher or person in authority attempted to discipline him. However, Arthur was considered so extraordinary in his creativity and intelligence that the school authorities overlooked any signs of difficulty such as chronic lateness, absence, and so forth. Arthur's writing was so outstanding that his stories and articles were published by a national journal featuring the creative achievements of homeless youth for which he won prizes and genuine recognition.

The content of his creative writing revealed the schizoid quality of his inner life. He described the family history as if they were living through the adventures of a Marx Brothers comedy and always coming out on top despite the formidable problems they encountered. The stories suggested that the family was comprised of ineffectual and silly, but well-meaning persons and he was the all-conquering hero who kept everyone afloat. There was certainly much truth to this description but it was also an idealization in that he greatly exaggerated his capacity to keep himself and the family afloat and also neglected to describe many instances in which the behavior of the adults may have been described as less than well-meaning. The adventures were written in a hysterically funny way, but also neglected to describe many of the painful incidents in his life in which he was deprived of food, lived in circumstances in which he was realistically endangered, and experienced severe neglect and abuse. The stories of his family closely resembled his long-ago play with cockroaches in which he would imprison them or set them free "for their own good." The fact that he pretended that the cockroaches were criminals reflected his rage at the parental objects for their not taking adequate care of him and his unconscious view of them as bad objects. His creative writing therefore reflected a manic defense in which he fantasized having omnipotent control over an ideal internal family. In this way, he defended against the pain and rage over the severe deprivation and chaos of his actual family life and personal history. Nevertheless, the schizoid withdrawal into phantasy served an adaptive function in allowing him to cope as best he could given that he was powerless to change his life and that therapy was unavailable. Therefore, he utilized his natural creativity and intelligence in the service of the manic defense in order to cope with his difficult circumstances. His efforts were effective enough to win him recognition and rewards from the larger community and to provide him with temporary relief from an untenable situation.

Nevertheless, Arthur's defensive efforts had negative ramifications that became apparent in his reactions to significant object loss. His grandmother died of a sudden heart attack in his early adolescence and then his mother, a drug addict, became ill with AIDS. Arthur remained detached in the face of both catastrophes. Attending his grandmother's funeral, he felt disconnected and unreal, as if he was living through an episode in a novel.

The detachment continued in the case of his mother's illness. When he visited her in the hospital, he observed the situation from the viewpoint of a writer. He observed her facial expressions, gestures, bodily movements, and any sign of pain in order to accurately describe how a person appears when dying.

Arthur's mother's condition deteriorated and he was placed in a foster group home. There his problems became apparent. The staff was concerned that Arthur could never ask anyone for help. He did not get along with peers because he always tried to boss them. He could not obey any rules and regulations especially in relation to the females in authority.

Arthur was referred to an inner-city clinic for a diagnostic assessment. He was able to maintain the schizoid phantasy of omnipotent control over the internal ideal family if external circumstances mirrored and reinforced the fantasy. Once he was placed in the group home, a situation where he was not in control as he had been in his family, he was threatened by this challenge to his schizoid defenses, which protected him from the pain and rage over the chaos of his familial and environmental situation. His anger at his mother and grandmother was displaced in his play with the criminal cockroaches and in his rebellion against the female authorities of the group home. Arthur's schizoid features had both adaptive and maladaptive components.

Roger was a middle-aged Caucasian patient and successful novelist who had grown up in a wealthy upper-class family. His parents were highly narcissistic and active socialites who spent little time with their only child. The parents were seldom at home and left Roger in the care of a governess. In the time that they spent with Roger, the parents were sporadic, overindulging him with material things but neglecting him emotionally. Therefore, the contacts with the parents were inevitably disappointing and gave rise to misbehavior on Roger's part with the governess as he displaced his anger. Roger was sent to boarding schools for his elementary and high school education. He excelled academically and won awards for outstanding achievement. He attended college abroad and upon graduation pursued a nomadic existence, moving around between the major cities but never settling permanently. Given the fact that he was well-off economically, he was not burdened by environmental difficulties and could afford to travel, live in the place of his choice, and devote himself to his writing. He thought of himself as a modern-day aristocrat and gentleman of leisure. The persons who knew him envied his ability to live wherever he chose, to pick himself up when he grew tired of a place, and to do whatever he wished with his life. Similarly, he lived a nomadic existence in romantic relationships, having a series of lovers but never sustaining a lasting relationship. Roger seemed to live as he pleased and did not appear unduly distressed about his life circumstances. He achieved a certain relative emotional stability in his life that he might not have accomplished if he had to struggle with making his own living or if he did not have the economic circumstances to permit him to live as he pleased.

Much of Roger's life centered around his writing. As a child, he had been an avid reader. He loved to read of adventures in faraway places and then fantasize about running away on such an adventure. Given his parents' penchant for travelling and living far from home, it is likely that Roger identified with them and fantasized of joining them on their adventures. Similarly, the fantasies of travel were a way to join the internal parents and to be with them in their travels.

In his own writings, Roger concentrated upon the complexities of relationships. The characters lived in his mind more fully and vitally than any of his relationships in reality. It was as if they lived out the story and he was more of a witness and transcriber than the author of events. He felt that he lived vicariously through the adventures of the characters of his books. When they came together in love, their union warmed his being. When one misunderstood the other, he felt the frustration and the wish for clarification. When one was abandoned, he himself experienced the sense of rejection. He might be engaged in an activity and not thinking of his writing when a character would intrude on his thoughts and continue the story.

Roger had always lived in his mind, absorbed in a rich fantasy life. In his relations to outer reality, he was an astute observer but not an active participant. He was especially interested in observing the subtleties and complexities of relationships, which then served to further stimulate his fantasy life. Guntrip (1969) has remarked that the schizoid patient, living predominantly in the internal world, is often insightful about human motivation and relationships. Roger's fantasy life was so vivid and rich that he sometimes could not distinguish it from reality. Thus, when he fantasized that a significant external object was injured, became ill, or was endangered, the associated affects were so intense and vivid that they overwhelmed his psychic life. The strength of Roger's fantasies were reflective of his involvement in the internal as opposed to external object world.

In his early childhood, Roger was provided with a "taste" of good object relations in the sporadic affection and attention he received from his parents and babysitters. However, their care was insufficient and inconsistent, resulting in traumatic disappointment. Roger gave up on the disappointing external objects and turned his longing to their internal counterparts. As a child, he was often left alone. He stimulated and entertained himself by his active and rich fantasy life. He was preoccupied with fantasies regarding his parents' life, their coupling, their activities and life apart from him. It was their absence that created this never-to-be-satisfied yearning to participate in their life. He re-created the childhood fantasies about his parents in the episodes about couples in his novels. He created scenes of family intimacy that reflected his own longing for a good object or ideal family.

There were also scenes that reflected his need and frustration at the hands of an exciting object or rejection in relationship to an abandoning object.

Schizoid states play an important part in the creative process in that the artist has considerable access to the internal object world which he then transforms, through secondary-process reworking, into the creative product. Dickens and Tolstoy experienced significant object loss in early life and then endeavored to compensate for disappointing external relationships by wish-fulfilling imaginary relationships that were later reflected in their creative writings (Wilson 1988). In fact, Klein was influenced in her discovery of the internal object world by the stream of consciousness narratives of James Joyce and Marcel Proust in which the subject's view of reality is colored and shaped by the internal world (Grosskurth 1986).

Roger was highly productive. Even when fatigued, depressed, or ill, he continued to write. He was aware of an inordinate need for recognition and acclaim to fill the void of early object loss. With the completion of each book, he became depressed. He felt no joy in success and experienced life as meaningless. In his state of nihilism, he thought of Yukio Mishima, the Japanese novelist who committed ritualistic suicide after completing *The Sea of Fertility* tetralogy.

After completing a creative activity following a period of prolonged pregnant absorption, it is not unusual or pathological for one to experience a temporary sense of emptiness and loss. However, the emptiness experienced by Roger was pervasive and pathological in the sense of reawakening the void of early object loss that the efforts of narcissistic aspiration could never fulfill. Nevertheless, Roger's schizoid states did have an adaptive side in providing him with a connection to objects even if they were primarily internal relationships.

Although Arthur and Roger came from entirely different socioeconomic circumstances, both patients endeavored to achieve omnipotent control over an ideal internal family to compensate for disappointments in external object relationships. It can also be seen that early object loss can give rise to strong narcissistic aspirations to fill the empty core.

DIRECT INTERPRETATION OF A SCHIZOID OBSESSION

The schizoid individual who represses the infantile frustrated longing to be loved eventually becomes discouraged and resigns himself to never being loved. Guntrip (1969) describes the active, needy, oral self undergoing a further split into a passive, regressed, withdrawn ego. It seems to me that in most cases, it is not necessary to posit a further splitting of the self. Rather, the needy infantile self simply becomes a hopeless, passive, regressed self that exerts a strong attraction toward the remaining personality, drawing it into irresistible ego regression. Guntrip (1969) states that it is at this point that the dread of the objectless state arises; the schizoid individual fears that in regression he will lose his internal as well as external object. He becomes fatigued, can barely function, and may desperately cling to the remaining vestiges of object relations. One female patient could barely drag herself through a day of work and collapsed after returning home each day. She had no energy to shop, cook, clean, or associate with friends. Her family and friends berated her for never returning their phone messages, but she was too fragile and fatigued to relate. The regressed self, withdrawing into an enclosed womblike state, draws the remaining personality into the quicksand of emotional collapse.

The withdrawing schizoid individual is threatened with losing both the inner and outer world of objects (Guntrip 1969) and may cling to an object as a drowning man clings to a life raft.

In Chapter 1, I discussed that the schizoid person primarily fears that he will destroy the external love object by draining him of his vital being. The person may effect a compromise by clinging to an internal as opposed to an external object. Frequently there will be a hyperlibidinal arousal that enables the individual to remain object related. Thus, the libidinal drive and the incestuous wish are used by the schizoid person to remain in contact with the object world. The patient threatened with object loss may stay connected through the obsessive libidinal fantasy of an object relationship. The fantasy may support a crippled ego by providing it with a crutch so that it does not collapse. A major difference between the schizoid and the borderline patient is that in the schizoid the obsessive fantasy is less related to reality and subject to greater distortion. It often remains a fantasy but on occasion it is acted out and has the potential to become bizarre and delusional and cross the border into a psychotic delusion.

One sometimes hears of a reclusive individual becoming obsessed with a celebrity. There may be a long duration where the "fan" restricts the obsession to remaining an exciting fantasy that prevents withdrawal and complete apathy toward life. However, there are occasions in which the individual crosses the line of fantasy and acts out the obsession, occasionally even with tragic consequences. It seems that the schizoid individual attempts to maintain the obsession on a fantasy level because he is aware that the need for love knows no bounds. The schizoid's need for love may become an overwhelming, sexualized, incestuous drive, the excitement of which wards off ego regression and stimulates a feeling of being alive. The schizoid's obsessive internal object love differs from that of the borderline patient, who enacts the internal relationship in the interpersonal arena in greater accord with reality. The borderline patient works hard through the use of projective identification to transform the outer object into an image of its inner counterpart. Furthermore, the borderline is not so overwhelmed with insatiable need. The borderline patient initially turns toward the object with insatiable need, eventually feels rejected, rejects the object in turn, and then fears object loss. Thus, the borderline is primarily concerned with destroying the object through aggressive distancing. It is the schizoid person who cannot accept rejection and may enact the internal obsession in the interpersonal domain without regard for reality. Typically, the schizoid endeavors to completely repress the hunger for love. As long as the repression is effective, he relates to the outer object world in a realistic but emotionally shallow manner. If the schizoid person is threatened with massive regressive withdrawal he may resort to an obsessive fatal attraction, desperately clinging to object relatedness.

THE CASE OF JOHN

This case illustrates the direct interpretive technique in helping a patient who oscillated between mad libidinal obsession and complete regressive withdrawal.

History

John was a single adult male living independently and employed full-time as an executive. His mother was domineering and abusive, his father was a manic-depressive. John recalled withdrawing into himself throughout his childhood to escape his mother's criticism. When she wasn't being critical she ignored him. The father was also removed and unrelated. John often felt alone in the family and stimulated himself with an active fantasy life, reading and watching television. He had few friends and was not comfortable with peers nor skillful at sports and games they played. A major theme of childhood was feeling left out.

In school he did not concentrate upon lessons or class discussion but was preoccupied with daydreams. He recalled that everybody described him as "living in his own world." A favorite fantasy reflected the internal splittings of his psychic states. He imagined escaping at will from the classroom into a secret subterranean tunnel. A go-cart awaited him. Then he imagined the teachers and students who hated him giving chase in the tunnel. On the panel of his cart were buttons that aimed deadly spears at his assailants. The flight into the tunnel reflected the regressive withdrawal inward of the active, needy self. The flight from interpersonal reality threatened him with object loss. Therefore, he had the persecutory objects (teachers, children) chase after him. After destroying the bad objects, he was threatened again with isolation. As he became older, he elaborated the fantasy. He returned to the world above, but now he was invisible. He situated himself behind the private rooms of the woman of his choice, to feast upon her visually, seeing her nakedness but unseen and unknown. Thus, the orally hungry self returned, but safely, with no danger of rejection or of being captured in the disapproving gaze of the exciting object.

John moved from the family home upon completing college. For a brief period, he experimented with drugs (mostly marijuana) and regularly visited prostitutes. On the one hand, he felt ashamed at having to pay for contact and the fulfillment of his sexual hunger. He was aware of the safety in these situations in that as long as he paid, the women did not reject him. He did not work steadily during this period and felt that he lived as a dissolute. Finally, worrying that he would never come to anything, he resolutely pledged to give up "drugs and whoring around" and "to knuckle under" to a steady job, and he started at his current position. For a time he was a workaholic, faithful to his pledge to give up drugs and prostitutes. He became increasingly lonely and fatigued. His only contact with people was at the job. He became overwhelmed with the need to be loved as well as a ravenous sexual hunger. He visited prostitutes but could no longer feel satisfied since he was aware that they were performing for a fee. He would approach women at bars and night spots but they rejected him. He felt that his hunger was apparent and frightened them away. He became obsessed with the idea of a warm, soft breast to lie upon and hungrily stared at the breasts of the women he saw in the street. In his longing for human warmth, he was aware of the concrete, asphalt stone city. It became a major effort to arise from bed to enter what he perceived as the labyrinth of urban daily life. He dragged himself to the train, a projectile hurled through the subterranean world, his body pressed against others. It seemed like a cruel joke as he recalled the imaginary tunnel of escape; his haven from the other world somehow transformed into a subway tunnel from which he emerged into the "real world." He was barely able to work and struggle against the overpowering longing to take to his bed and hide beneath the covers.

The Obsessions

John was in an exhausted state at the time a young woman came to work as his secretary. She was pretty and engaging. She offered to make coffee, dust his desk, and run errands. She admired his efficacy, assurance, and other traits. He felt profoundly grateful.

Thus, the secretary was for John a libidinally exciting object that awakened him to living. Thinking of her, he had a reason to get out of bed each day. She was primarily a subjective object (Winnicott 1963) for John in the sense that he felt that she had been created and sent from heaven to rescue him from his desolate life. On the train, thinking of Liz, he was oblivious to the grime and the human throng. In his mind, he rested upon her soft, warm breast. All that he saw before him was the space separating him from his love object. The skyscrapers and urban blight were now only landmarks by which he read his proximity to Liz. No longer did he feel surrounded by the desolate, unyielding city of stone and asphalt. He thought of Liz every waking moment. Once he asked her out. She replied that he was attractive and interesting but that she was going through a difficult divorce and did not wish to date. He settled for this answer. In his mind, they were in love and both were pained that circumstances did not allow for them to be together. Believing this, he could be in love with his love for Liz. On some level, he was aware that she did not know the extent of his feelings but this pleased him. It was similar to his fantasy of being in the private rooms of a woman, and seeing her nakedness.

He wrote Liz complimentary notes about a letter she had dictated, her radiant smile, her lovely dress. These notes rather quickly changed into thinly veiled love letters. John was stunned when his boss informed him that Liz was to be transferred to another division of the company although this was a usual company practice. He would see her daily but she would no longer work for him. He ardently protested and realized that the boss must have puzzled over his agitation. He was astonished when he asked Liz herself to protest and she replied that she would miss working for him but she did not want to make a fuss.

John now felt persecuted and troubled by his obsessive love for Liz. He felt she had betrayed him. He thought she pretended to return his love in order to take advantage of him. He imagined that she was laughing at him for being a fool. Things went from bad to worse when he learned that she was dating a man outside of the office. John approached her and said that since she is over her divorce, she owed him a date. She replied that she thought it best not to date someone in the office. He wanted to crush her, belittle her, throw her upon the floor and rape and sodomize her. He thought about following her home and spying on the man she dated. He was afraid to lose control. He feared he might act inappropriately and have an outburst at work or that if he restrained himself, he might do something even crazier afterwards. At this point, he went for a consultation with a female therapist. She was understandably concerned about his potential for a psychotic transference toward a female. She referred him to me.

Treatment

When John first came in to see me, he was distraught. He wrung his hands and pleaded "What can I do? She is destroying me." Yet I was somewhat hopeful in that even with the severity of his disorder, he was definite that he did not want to act out on his destructive impulses and he wanted help with the obsession. I believe the prognosis would have been significantly worse if he only wanted help in fulfilling his fantasy and winning Liz. In the first interview, when he was calm, he recognized that he exaggerated the significance of the romantic aspects of their relationship. He said "We were just two people working together, but for me it was as if she were my office wife. This relationship meant much more to me than it did to her. Don't get me wrong. She didn't love me. She may have been attracted to me, but I sometimes felt that we were in love. This is not where she was at but at the time, I did not always know. I believed it meant more to her."

However, as John continued to talk, he was emotionally carried away and would confuse his fantasies with reality. He said that Liz had deliberately deceived him, feigning love to take advantage, to humiliate him.

Schizoid patients often relate to others most comfortably in an abstract, intellectual manner. One of the only characteristics that John ever described with narcissistic pleasure was his capacity to intellectualize and analyze. It seemed that John sometimes managed to moderate his overwhelming dependency needs by relating in an intellectual, logical fashion. His distress about Liz sporadically disturbed his dispassionate intellectualizing.

Initially, I responded to John by joining in the intellectualizing about his problems with Liz in order to engage him in a nonthreatening fashion that supported the higher-level defense. John felt humiliated by his belief that Liz had fooled him into believing that she provided him with favors such as compliments, coffee, and the dusting of his desk because she loved him. When he thought of her as laughing at him for returning her favors by allowing her to come in to work late, leave early, and so forth, he wanted to injure her.

I intervened by describing the situation in its barest objective essentials distinguishing the actual events from what John made of them in his mind. Thus, I said, "What we know is that as your secretary Liz provided coffee, compliments, and so forth, which is more than any other secretary did for you in the line of duty. Feeling grateful, you provided her with favors in return, allowing her to come in late, leave early, and so forth. You also asked her out and she said she liked you but did not want to go out because she was going through a divorce and then later because she did not want to mix business with pleasure. This is what we know—what Liz has told you and what you have told me—is that correct?" He acknowledged it was and then I remarked on what he has made out of these events in his mind. "You fantasized that Liz provided you with favors because she loved you—you created a loving Liz in your mind that may or may not accord with the actual Liz. Then once you were disappointed and hurt you went a step further and created an image of Liz feigning love in order to fool you into providing favors. Thus, you have created a deceitful Liz, whom you now hate and wish to destroy."

I continually pointed out that there were the actual events and what John created out of these events, and that the creation was a subjective Liz that lived in his mind as opposed to the external, objective Liz. It was emphasized that we could not be

. certain of the actual meaning of events or motivations of Liz with the little information available. His fantasy might by some chance be an accurate interpretation of the events but other fantasies or explanations might be equally or even more plausible. These interventions resulted in John allowing himself to entertain other plausible speculations about Liz's behavior. For instance, he thought further about how she had been going through a difficult divorce when they had first met and he wondered if she might have provided John with "favors" because of her own need to feel appreciated by a man given the mutual rejection occurring in her relationship with her husband. Therefore, as John was able to free himself of the preoccupying subjective fantasy of Liz feigning love, he considered other plausible possibilities and endeavored to arrive at a more objectively perceived object.

These reality-oriented interventions did not in themselves significantly modify John's personality structure. However, they did serve to calm him and lessen his rage toward Liz and himself. In viewing Liz as tricking him into believing she loved him, John felt humiliated and hated himself. The self-hate lessened as John began to realize that Liz had her own motivations, interests, and wishes separate from her feelings about him. However, as Winnicott (1963) points out, the recognition of the objectively perceived object is a gradual process requiring continual working-through in treatment.

John discussed a problem that is common for schizoid patients. He was never sure of how to read other people's social cues. I remarked that he initially read Liz's warmth and favors through his own longing to be loved. He held on to this thought to lessen his feelings of humiliation and vengeful thoughts toward Liz.

The Therapeutic Dilemma

The therapy of patients such as John poses a treatment dilemma. There is the serious threat that the obsessional fantasy could slip into a full-blown psychotic delusion with the threat of acting out or even violence. At the same time the obsession does serve a positive function in keeping the patient in contact with the object world, although in a bizarre fashion. Earlier, I remarked upon John's obsession with breasts. Guntrip (1969) described a patient who had an identical symptom and when he interpreted it in terms of regression to orality, this patient slipped into a complete schizoid withdrawal. The obsession with the earliest object was not primarily a regression but rather the patient's last effort to remain object related. John's obsessive fantasies served the same function. The direct interpretative technique aims toward distinguishing fantasy from reality and the subjective from the objective object while helping the patient remain object related. Enabling the patient to begin to distinguish the subjective nature of the object is a priority given the threat that the fantasy could become a full-blown delusion with destructive consequences. However, as the patient gradually differentiates the subjective and objective realms, the therapist supports the object relational value of the obsessive symptom.

Distinguishing Fantasy from Reality

John reported that when he entered work one morning, Liz was leaning over her desk working on a report. John said good morning. She glanced up, nodded, and returned to her work. John went into his office devastated. He could not work, return calls, or talk to anyone.

In such a situation, the therapist might mistakenly think that it would be empathic to express understanding for the fact that John feels hurt, angry, or rejected by Liz. Therapists sometimes make the mistake of responding empathically to obsessions that are less apparently fantastic and seem based on actual occurrences but are primarily schizoid and based on fantasy and a relationship to the subjective object. Such interventions are not truly empathic because they reinforce the patient's belief that he is worthless. This is because John conceives of Liz primarily as a subjective object who exists exclusively in relation to his needs. If she greets him warmly it is because he is worthy and if she merely nods, it is because he is unworthy. In his mind, whatever she does is always based on him, never upon her own separate motivations, interests, and so forth. She is either for or against him in all of her actions. John could not conceive that she merely nodded and returned to the report because she was absorbed by her work. In his mind, the quick nod meant she felt negatively about him.

I intervened by painting a verbal picture of the events that juxtaposed the event itself with John's strong reaction. I included only the bare essentials of the situation, leaving out all of the patient's projections in order to demonstrate that the event itself does not warrant the reaction. I said "Let's see if I have this right. You enter the office, Liz is busy working—leaning over a report, if I remember. You say 'hi,' she looks up, nods, returns to the report. You go into your office depressed and immobilized, unable to work all day. Is that correct?"

"Yes . . . when you describe it that way, it seems like nothing happened. We just say 'hi' to one another and I fall apart."

"Yes, exactly. That's exactly what you said—true? That's why I repeated it. I don't understand your reaction. It's not self-evident in terms of what occurred."

"No—it's not about what occurred. No. I mean it's not just about saying 'hi' to one another or a nod. It's about what I feel about her, what is happening inside about it."

"Yes," I said, "That is what I thought we should look at. What is happening in your mind. Not just the event, because your reaction seems related to what is occurring inside, as opposed to the event itself."

John described how he thought of Liz every moment of the weekend, longing for Monday and their reunion. Thinking of Liz gave him something to live for but also drove him crazy. In his thoughts, he told her all about his feelings toward her.

I replied how "there are two relationships with Liz. There is the subjective relationship with Liz in your mind. You were with the subjective Liz all weekend. She knew every thought and feeling in your mind just by virtue of being thought of by you. You return to work on Monday and there is Liz acting as if she hardly knows you. She sits at her desk, working on her report—she has not heard one thought you have had all weekend. She acts as if her only concern is the report in front of her that she must finish. She looks when you say 'hi' as if it distracts her from this job she must finish. Thus you have two relationships with Liz. One is subjective, the Liz that you created, a witness to whom you bare every thought and feeling in your soul and who exists only for you. This is the subjective Liz whom you expected to find waiting around at work. Then there is Liz as she is who is not a part of your fantasy but living her own life, typing her report, not knowing your thoughts this weekend."

In this way, through similar repeated episodes I engaged John in distinguishing the subjective from the objective object. I also interpreted John's fantasy that he was rejected. "After Liz nodded, you went into your office and mourned. This is part of your fantasy too. That you are a jilted lover. You are genuinely feeling the emotions but in relationship to the fantasy."

He replied, "Whenever I am undergoing this, I feel like a character in a film, or novel. I had that thought when I was upset in my office. I imagined that this was a movie and then I thought of a scene in which I would get drunk and be lying face down on the bar, my drink in hand."

The schizoid individual often has an unreal sense of being a character in a play, novel, or film and this reflects living in an inner fantasy world. The idea that he is being watched refers to the early need to be mirrored by the object. He is especially in need of mirroring when he is withdrawn and struggling to remain in contact. Thus his fantasy was a play within the play of office life and he created the fantasy to keep functioning. When John experienced destructive impulses toward himself or Liz, I directly stated that belief in the fantasy was craziness. Thus I referred to John's obsession as "Liz madness." He found himself repeating this phrase at work whenever he feared the obsession might overwhelm him. He would say to himself "You are being consumed again by Liz madness." I said he should try to maintain the therapeutic relationship in mind as a buffer to the Liz madness.

Empathizing with the Need for Contact

Only after the patient is able to consistently distinguish reality and fantasy, do I address the adaptive aspect of the fantasy. I reminded John that before he had met Liz he felt like collapsing and could barely go to work. It was explained that for some reason, he found the need for people dangerous, so he had withdrawn. The further he removed himself, the more isolated and depressed he became. Liz appeared and he felt that she took care of him in her function as secretary. I listed all she had done that pleased him and pointed out that she had mothered him. His earlier statement that Liz was his office wife was translated into Liz was his office mother. He became quite embarrassed that, as a grown man, he should need a mother. I asked for associations. He said he felt like a mama's boy. He recalled that throughout his childhood and youth, it was important to avoid even being thought of as a mama's boy.

I asked about the relationship between his parents, and he replied that his mother was abusive and neglectful and that his father was depressed and withdrawn. I interpreted that he gave up on receiving the parenting he needed for growth at a very early age and turned inward for stimulation. The childhood fantasy of the escape to the subterranean tunnel symbolized the withdrawal to the inner world. Nevertheless, he needed the mother and therefore returned invisible to "feast" on the nakedness of women. I interpreted that this was a wish to see but not be seen by the mother, to transform her into his "object" instead of becoming her object.

His mother was critical and abusive to him in order to control him. Thus he fantasized being invisible so that she could neither see, control, nor objectify him. In this way, he attempted to protect the secret, core self (Winnicott 1963) from impingement and violation. These interventions provided a framework for me to state, "You withdrew from the abuse and neglect of your parents. You increasingly felt alone, isolated and lacked any enthusiasm for life. You had given up on receiving anything from people. Still, no matter how much you withdrew, you could not deny your need for relationships. You hungrily gazed at all of the breasts to keep yourself related and connected to something human. You longed for a soft, warm breast but were constantly aware of being surrounded by the cold, stone city. You have described your mother as hard, unyielding, cold. Your consciousness of the asphalt, concrete, stone city referred to the image of the hard and cold mother who filled your mind. You could only withdraw from the stone mother. You wanted to retreat from living and take to the bed. You wanted a soft, warm, nurturing breast, not a stone breast. Then Liz appeared. When she was nurturing and warm, you felt mothered. She gave you something to live for. You could endure the stone city, knowing Liz was at the other end. She was your goal. She excited you. She aroused you from your bed and your withdrawn state. She became your reason for being. You turned on to get to her. This is the way it is with a baby and mother. The mother's holding excites the baby. The pleasure turns the baby on, gets it going, gives it a reason to be. Given the emptiness and exhaustion you felt, you became addicted to Liz as your reason to be."

I reiterated this over a couple of sessions. He was fascinated, wide eyed, taking in the words. John was in constant dread of the collapse of his personality based upon the basic fault or deficient psychic structure resulting from the failure of primary love (Balint 1968). The addiction to Liz served to compensate for his inner emptiness. I empathized with his inner emptiness and consequent desperate need for object contact.

Accepting the Freedom of the Object

The sessions now involved working through. John would discuss incidents of jealousy. He was upset when he saw Liz at lunch with her boyfriend, when she spoke to anyone else, if she read a book instead of talking to him. He became quite upset in sessions, and sometimes in agitation screamed, "She has no right to ignore me. She should not be with the boyfriend. I have thoughts of killing them. I thought of yanking the book out of her hand. I hate to see her involved with anything but me."

At times he was self-righteous and claimed the right to control her. I remarked that his complaints boiled down to not being able to control Liz's attention. The therapist said, "You long to be her only object of desire. You become uncontrollably jealous whenever she has any other object of interest ranging from a report, to work, to her boyfriend. She has a right to freely choose her interests. What you are experiencing toward Liz are the feelings of a baby wanting to be its mother's sole object of desire and not being able to tolerate the mother giving attention to the father, her own interests, or other people. Liz directing her attention elsewhere is for you the living out or the reliving of a baby discovering the mother's freedom to direct attention where she pleases."

He spoke of how his mother only gave him attention when he misbehaved or when she felt the inclination for contact regardless of his needs. He was often invisible for her. She always read and he felt insanely jealous. I said that his demand for Liz to give him undivided attention, his belief in his right to it, actually referred to his mother, not to Liz, and to a baby's right to be the object of the mother's desire.

Winnicott (1963) states that in the first weeks of life, the infant experiences absolute dependence on the caregiver, who in turn is fully identified with the infant in primary maternal preoccupation. Fairbairn (1944) suggested an initial vague but rudimentary knowledge of self and other on the part of the infant. Thus, the mother's primary maternal identification and fitting herself into the needs of the infant prevent this initial knowledge of separation from becoming overwhelming in that the infant fantasizes that he creates a subjective object exclusively devoted to him (Winnicott 1963). It is only after this experience of symbiotic union that the infant can tolerate the parent's failures in meeting its needs and the knowledge that the mother has objects of desire other than the infant. In fact, Winnicott states that in this phase of relative dependence, it is essential for the infant's individuation that the mother gradually returns to other interests and sometimes fails the child.

> John's desperate need to be the only object of desire for Liz and his obsessive jealousy of her other interests suggest that he experienced traumatic failure in the earliest phase of absolute dependence and was therefore still struggling to create the subjective object exclusively devoted to him. He longed to be looked upon by his mother, but when she did see him it was always critically. He sometimes misbehaved because it was better to be seen negatively than not at all. The fantasy of being invisible and feasting his eyes on a naked woman was an expression of his active need to greedily devour the object, a hunger that had grown in proportion to his need not to be seen or devoured by the impinging object. Winnicott suggests that failure in the earliest, passive need to be loved and held is compensated for by the active, orally greedy need to love and to devour.

Incestuous Desire and an Expression of the Need for Love

> John also discussed what he referred to as his "insane desire" for Liz. He stated that when they first met, he did not find her unusually attractive. She became more desirable in proportion to his emotional dependence upon her. He said, "I walk

around with a hard-on all day thinking of her. I can't think of anything else. She has become the most desirable woman in the world to me. I want to penetrate her. It doesn't matter where. I will settle for any hole in her body. I'm becoming a madman."

I related the intensity of John's arousal to the dependency on Liz for mothering. John laughed and said that sex with Liz would cure him. He asked if it were an Oedipus complex. I responded that the intensity of the sexual wish for Liz was related to an incestuous wish. John said he was sometimes very upset because of masturbatory fantasies about his mother. He said most of his sexual fantasies had to do with raping and beating women. There was one typical fantasy in which he raped a woman and made her moan with desire. The key element common to all of the fantasies was the forcing of the woman to desire him and penetrating her so that she looked at him with desire in her eyes.

I interpreted, "Through sex you force the mother image to look at you. The longing to be looked upon to confirm your existence so that you will not be invisible is manifested in the sexual fantasy. You make the mothering face look on you with desire and therefore make yourself into her object of desire. The need to be loved by your mother has been frustrated. The strong wish for incest has taken its place. The natural sensual feelings a child feels in relation to the closeness with the mother that culminate in the wish to possess or marry the mother have become for you an obsession to compensate for your mother not loving you enough. Ordinarily the sensual feelings toward the parent figures are a part of the overall relationship bringing child and parent closer in love and serving bonding. In your case the bond failed and you perceived your mother as made of stone, impregnable, hard, so there is the desire to penetrate her, to get under her skin, to make her take notice of you. The incestuous wish is the only way you can make contact in your fantasy. Also, you yourself cannot gratify your wish to be loved by her. That is in her power but you can gratify the sexual wish yourself through masturbation. In the sexual fantasy you can control the internal mother."

I explained that John would not permit himself to become erotically obsessed with his mother; his sense of reality and morality prohibited no more than a fleeting breaking through of fantasy. However, much of his hostility and fantasies of dominance over women was based upon the frustrated need for mothering. John first responded with astonishment to these interpretations and sometimes expressed disbelief. For instance, he would say, "So my wish to rape Liz is not just because she is so desirable?"

I replied, "She may be desirable and you could well be attracted to her for herself but in addition to a basic attraction there is an obsession going on that is much more."

He could see that but would argue briefly, then associate with further convincing evidence supporting what I had said, for instance, recalling his incestuous masturbatory fantasies.

Some of the direct interpretations may seem bold but they are necessary to address the patient's difficulties. Therapists listening to case examples of direct object relationship interpretations made in the first months of treatment sometimes wonder whether it is problematic to interpret the patient's incestuous wishes early on. I hold that it is more problematic for a patient like John to believe that his sadistic and domineering fantasies are being aroused only by the women themselves. After an initial brief period of resistance, John felt relieved to realize that Liz was not primarily responsible for all of his feelings. At the end of the session, he would sometimes actually ask for reassurance, saying, "So this is not just about Liz. It's about my need for mothering. It's about incest as an expression of that need."

I have found that patients are able to take in and use direct interpretations about instinctual drives, incestuous wishes, sadism, greed, and envy when these issues are discussed in terms of serving the need for object love or compensating for failures in object relating. The theories of Balint, Fairbairn, Guntrip, and Winnicott permit the therapist to empathize with the actual infantile developmental failures, impasses, and needs. John's initial belief that his problems centered around Liz rejecting him defended him from the realization that his difficulties related to the basic fault, failures in primary love and the addictive need for love to compensate for inner emptiness. Empathizing with John's depression over rejection by Liz would not have been true empathy but instead reinforced his sense of unworthiness and his belief that all of Liz's behavior was either for or against him. Object relations theory and its implications for technique allow the therapist to interpret the subjective nature of the object and then to empathize with the empty core resulting from the failure in primary love in early life.

Addressing John's Striving to Become the Object of Desire

John was seen in once-weekly treatment for about four months when the obsession with Liz began to significantly subside. He then spoke of how lonely and isolated he was and how he longed to have sex and closeness with a woman, but he made no active efforts to meet any women. I remarked that as lonely as he felt, he did not initiate contact with others. I made it clear that I was not suggesting that John should meet people, nor was I castigating him. I suggested he might be better off not meeting people at this time. What was being addressed was that as much as he said he wanted to meet people, maybe he really wanted to be alone, and if so, it should at least be discussed so that he becomes more aware of the different sides of himself.

John replied that he didn't think it was just that he wanted to be alone. He didn't want to initiate a relationship with a woman. He wanted others to seek him out. He wanted a woman to see him and be turned on and go after him. I remarked that he wanted to be the object of the woman's desire. He said he wanted a woman to want him, to jump all over him, to rape him. I said that he was expressing his wish to be loved by his mother. What was most important in what he said was the wish to be "wanted." He longed to be a wanted baby. He had always felt like an invisible unwanted baby. He was expressing all of this in sexual terms, the wish to be wanted sexually. He became emotionally excited and said, "I see what you're saying. I would get attention if they raped me—I'd get so much attention. Yes."

Balint (1968) states that primary love is experienced by the infant passively, as the need to be loved and cared for. John's need for primary love was sexualized. The intensity and desperateness of that need were evidence of the basic fault or deficiency in psychic structure. As John became aware of the "subjective object" relationship, he was able to perceive Liz more objectively and to describe the strengths and weaknesses of her personality in their own right and not only in terms of relation to himself and his needs.

HYSTERIA, THE OEDIPUS CONFLICT, AND SCHIZOID STATES

Fairbairn (1941) notes that the hysterical personality and oedipal conflicts sometimes serve to defend against schizoid states. In John's case, the incestuous drive occurred over the schizoid empty core and the need for love.

A female young adult patient, Joan, had been emotionally deprived and grossly neglected by both of her parents. Throughout her childhood, she was preoccupied with oedipally oriented daydreams. She would spend hours fantasizing that she was kidnapped by Arabian Knights and had a love affair with one of her kidnappers. The oedipal fantasies filled the empty core and provided her with a rich, stimulating inner life to compensate for her loneliness. She then developed symptoms around a fear of germs, self-reproaches for her dirtiness, and dirty thoughts. She attributes her parents' neglect of her to her "dirty" forbidden oedipal striving. The parents were not available because of their own difficulties. It pained her more to think that her parents simply could not love her. A baby can only understand a parent's failure to love on the basis of the baby being unlovable, unworthy. For this patient it was safer to think her parents were punishing her because of her forbidden, incestuous, and rivalrous impulses.

When she later became involved in a close relationship with a boyfriend, she always imagined that he was interested in another female. Even when they watched television, she became threatened if an attractive actress appeared. The therapist first interpreted on the oedipal level that Joan punished herself for the oedipal triumph of winning the boyfriend by fantasizing about the other female, the mother, stealing him from her. This interpretation did not resolve the symptom. On a more basic level, Joan related to the boyfriend as a primary caregiver and sought mothering in their relationship. The need for maternal care was cast in oedipal romantic terms to make it more acceptable to the adult eye. The jealousy over other females reflected her wish to be the boyfriend's only object of desire and the incapacity to tolerate him having any other objects of interest. At the same time, the schizoid individual is terrified of closeness and seeks to couple the love object with third parties to create some separateness. Thus, the schizoid is caught between these conflicting wishes. The therapist must directly interpret these object relational issues to provide the patient with the opportunity to engage in and improve his object relationships.

4

DISSOCIATION IN MULTIPLE SELF STATES

Fairbairn's theory of the splitting of the self into multiple self states is based upon principles of modern biology. He views development in terms of the self undergoing differentiation as a result of encounters with the environment (Fairbairn 1946, 1949, 1951). In structuring early experience, a central self splits off painful experience around specific figures as incompatible with the affective inclinations of the central self (Sutherland 1989). Fairbairn perceives of the self as originally cohesive and actively structuring experience. Two sub-self systems become organized as the result of frustrated needs, one of which is a dependent self attempting to find satisfaction through its capacity to create images of the object. The other self is an anti-relational self that is identified with the rejecting responses of the caregiver toward infantile dependency needs. As Sutherland points out, the sub-selves have restricted aims but are selves in their own right as parts of the open self system. In describing Fairbairn's split-off selves as dynamic, active sub-selves, Sutherland has translated his theory into the terms of contemporary infant research. Stern has acknowledged that Fairbairn's work anticipated the current research findings.

The sub-selves of Fairbairn's theory have a reciprocal, dynamic, and active relationship. An internal saboteur, which I refer to as the anti-relational self, aggressively rejects the infantile, dependent self and its love objects. The sub-selves become dissociated from one another but there is a sense of wholeness and a central agent organizing overall experience. It seems that a major characteristic of severe psychopathology is that the central, active, organizing agent becomes lost in the chaos of fragmentation. Therefore, it becomes the initial task of the therapist to draw the active, organizing agent self (the synthetic function in ego psychological terms) into a central position. The therapist aims toward integration from fragmentation. It is understood that multiple sub-selves are normal and inevitable so the therapist does not aim for entirely eliminating splitting but rather strengthening the central organizing function.

Fairbairn's interest in dissociated psychic states can be traced back to his dissertation (1929) titled "The Relationship of Dissociation and Repression, Considered from the Point of View of Medical Psychology." Fairbairn's thesis, submitted toward the postgraduate degree of doctor of medicine, compared the contributions of Janet and Freud. Fairbairn rejected the common use of the terms repression and dissociation as interchangeable. Instead, he concluded that repression occurred on the highest level of psychic structure, the conceptual level of development, whereas dissociation related to segments of the psychic structure that were felt to be unpleasant to the organization of the self. Dissociation referred to unpleasurable external experience whereas repression had its roots in instinctual tensions (Sutherland 1989).

There are important issues of identification of dissociated self states in the patient's clinical narrative. Therapeutic interventions will be described that elicit and strengthen the pa-

tient's central organizational function. The therapist attempts
to bring forth the wholeness that exists in the background.

THE DISSOCIATED ANTI-RELATIONAL SELF

The Case of Bruce

Bruce is the young attorney I briefly described in Chapter 1.
He entered therapy because he felt uncomfortable in relationships, especially with females. Shortly after beginning treatment, he reported a dream. He tried to telephone two college
friends, a male and female. Neither was home. His associations
were that the female was an emotionally receptive friend, one
he could confide in. The male was a tried-and-true loyal
"buddy." He associated further that he did not see why he
would have to dream of calling either since, if he wished, he
could do so readily in reality.

Dream interpretation from a British object relations perspective is often constituted by identifying the sub-self structures and their dynamic relationship. I remarked that the self
Bruce was conscious of wanted to make contact with the
receptive friends. However, another self Bruce was unconscious of sabotaged his own efforts to make contact. Thus the
saboteur self removed the friends from the other end of the
phone line, arranging for them not to be at home to take the
calls. Bruce saw that the dream reflected his central problem:
he wished to have significant relationships, but some part of
him, unbeknownst to himself, thwarted his efforts.

He met a woman that he liked. He became afraid that he
would unconsciously sabotage his wish for a close, meaningful relationship. There were a number of occasions when
for no apparent reason, he became insecure about whether the
woman really cared for him. He pressured her for reassurance
in a manner that seemed to push her away. I carefully explored
what occurred preceding each episode of insecurity. It became
apparent that on each occasion, she had given him some
indication of her willingness to become further involved.

When he originally described the events, he omitted her small overtures, which seemed to him unrelated at the time. Thus, he projected the anti-relational self by experiencing the vague sense that she was becoming less interested or would become less involved, and then acting out on his insecurity. When he became conscious of the dissociated anti-relational self, he was able to reexamine former situations in which he broke off the relationship, imagining the other person was losing interest when it was actually he who could not tolerate closeness.

Becoming aware of the anti-relational self, he reported the following dream. He was in a taxicab going to the family's home where he had grown up. He was surprised the taxi driver knew the way because usually he had to direct the driver. He tried to engage the driver in discussion, but he responded with monosyllables and stuttering. The patient recalled that he had stuttered on occasion as a child. He took a closer look at the driver, who was ugly, slovenly, and overweight. The patient began to direct the driver even though they were only blocks away. The patient awakened.

Bruce associated that the driver was noncommunicative, slovenly, and overweight, and he felt this way about himself at different times in his life. The taxi driver represented a reserved, uncommunicative self state. He felt that he was afraid that this anti-relational self might take over the control of his personality. It was this self who did the driving while he was just the passenger. He tried to direct the driver, who would not listen because he knew how to reach the destination. The fearful patient wondered whether the parent's home of his childhood was symbolic of regression.

The Case of Esther

Esther illustrates the dissociation of the anti-relational self. This young adult female was employed in finance and came to treatment following the ending of a relationship. She had been in love but her clinging dependency pushed her boyfriend away. He was a psychologist and analyzed her (not professionally). She generally accepted his view of her problems. She lived alone and had a lucrative and rewarding job, but felt incomplete and longed for a relationship. She would come in each week complaining of her lack of contact with friends. There were never any telephone calls on the answering machine. Over time, the therapist silently observed that when a friend did invite her out, she did not go and that she never telephoned her friends. In sessions she repeatedly criticized herself for her dependent behavior. I replied, "The wish for a good relationship in which you are loved as a person in your own right is a natural need. If the need is disappointed it becomes urgent and demanding. There is a certain frustration point where it is inevitable that that need will become greed."

She had listened attentively and was responsive to this idea so I continued, "In a sense, you are in a double-bind situation. You cling so desperately out of repeated disappointments, but the very clinging, which can't always be helped, defeats its purpose by pushing the other person away."

She felt understood by me through these interpretations, which were responsive to the relational subjective component of her conflict. She then said that there may be more to it. She noticed that she tended to be attracted to men who are unavailable. She provided new information that indicated that the former boyfriend might have had some of his own difficulties around issues of intimacy. She then said that whenever a man seemed to be genuinely interested in her, the feelings were not reciprocal. Thus, in feeling understood by the therapist in the need for a healthy relationship, she was then able to reveal the anti-relational self.

THE MULTIPLICITY OF SELVES

The Case of Lillian

How the therapist can detect in the clinical narrative the multiplicity of selves in dynamic interaction is illustrated in the next case. Klein (1929) described how the child uses toys, dolls, materials, and the play setting to personify the internal object world. Similarly, the adult schizoid patient may utilize the narration of people and events in his daily life to personify his internal self and object world.

Lillian was a single parent and junior high school teacher who sought therapy because of an incapacity to be involved emotionally in relationships. Similar to Estelle, discussed in Chapter 10, Lillian was always on the giving end in relationships and in her professional life. She was known as the "earth mother." She was disturbed because she noticed that if other people were not suffering, she felt indifferent toward them. A recent boyfriend had also complained that she played at being lady bountiful in a relationship but could not engage in an equal give-and-take. These experiences precipitated her entry into treatment.

Lillian grew up in an intact but troubled family. The mother was schizophrenic, the father physically ailing, the older sister manic-depressive. Lillian literally held the family together by her exuberant attitude, her organizational ability, and sheer hard work. When not assuming a managerial family role, she withdrew into a solitary world of reading and writing fiction. She was disinterested in contact with peers. Her withdrawal was not noticed because of her outgoing behavior and abilities to relate to others through role-playing and to accomplish tasks. She was a talented writer, winning an award for fiction writing by a national magazine.

The patient reported the following situation, reflecting her internal multiplicity of selves. A highly respected teacher, Lillian consulted one day weekly at an inner-city school; she was a junior member in a team of consultants who provided training to teachers. Lillian complained of receiving virtually no help from the other consultants, who wanted to participate minimally. Lillian was troubled by her inability to be effectual in this impossible assignment. She became despondent over a young, inexperienced, and genuinely devoted female teacher who was neglected by both the school and consulting staff. The young teacher and her pupils had designed an art project.

The school administration hung it in a dark, out-of-the-way corner. The teacher had become increasingly depressed and planned to leave at the end of the academic year.

The dissociation of a sub-self state is evidenced when an individual does not present a specific affective state but experiences understanding or animosity for others who do experience this affective state. Borderline patients often merge with outer objects but on some level remain aware of the merger. For instance, a severely deprived borderline mother provided stray animals with the care she herself never received. She remained preconsciously aware that she was nurtured through her care of animals. She said that while nurturing them, she felt united and at one with them. The schizoid patient disowns the self state that is attributed to the other person.

Lillian experienced a dissociation of her infantile, frustrated, helpless self but became involved with persons, such as the young teacher, who displayed the affect states that Lillian never allowed herself to experience.

When I raised the possibility that this teacher might represent a denied, frustrated needy side of herself, she replied that it was not possible. For one thing the teacher was planning to quit and Lillian never quit anything. Secondly, the teacher (rightfully) blamed other people for her problems, whereas Lillian could never hold anyone but herself responsible given her level of experience, ability, and skill.

I questioned that Lillian never held anyone accountable but herself, wondering if she did not take on too much of this responsibility and whether it was entirely her responsibility that she could not do her job given what she reported about the lack of support from the consultation team and school administration. Lillian acknowledged that she did not get support, that she was not responsible for the failure. She started to describe the many ways that she was realistically thwarted. She went into a tirade about all the corruption of the administration and then fantasized about secretly bringing a tape recording to the next meeting and exposing the corruption. She then became despondent and said since she cannot fight, she might as well quit. She now became aware of the two affective states she had initially denied in relation to the young teacher: she spontaneously recalled having said that she would never quit (which she now felt like doing), and that she would never blame anyone but herself (she now felt the entire gang should be imprisoned.) Lillian was astounded that her feelings were similar to the teacher's. She acknowledged that she may have been disowning these feelings. She wished to know more about how this worked.

Lillian associated that she always denied negative feelings and conducted herself like a zealous young child who comes home from school and fervently prods the family to carry on and look alive. I asked her to associate to that idea. She said at home, she had always been the enthusiastic, optimistic child, driving out the family demons and ardently encouraging her catatonic mother, ailing father, and depressed sister to cheerfully carry on a normal family life.

I remarked, "As a child you buzzed about enthusiastically like a bee, injecting life into everyone. The only way you could maintain the smiling facade was to place the needy, helpless, frustrated part of yourself in an inaccessible corner. This was the way you felt when the school administration placed the project of the young teacher and pupils in a dark, removed corner. The project represented your helpless self, hidden away in the corner by your own internal administration, a parental part of your personality telling you to surrender your own needs and take care of everyone else." For the first time in the long period that I had treated this patient, she had a strong emotional reaction to my remarks. She visibly wept and acknowledged that as a child, she recalled talking to herself in a stern, admonishing parental voice that said, "whistle a happy tune and wipe the frown from your face."

The Dissociated Infantile Self—The Case of Marilyn

The following vignette illustrates how the therapist identifies and interprets the dissociated infantile self. I have discussed this patient, Marilyn (Seinfeld 1990) from the point of view of the tie to the bad object.

Marilyn, a middle-aged woman, was an only child. Her mother died from a stroke when she was four. She was left in the care of an insensitive, self-absorbed father and narcissistic grandmother. Marilyn became her own caretaker from a very early age and was placed in a parental position. She did not relate like a child but appeared to be playing the role of a stern kindergarten teacher. She grew up compulsively driven to function. The bitterness over her difficult life was the fuel that kept her going. She had struggled to finish college, establish a profession, and marry. None of her achievements enlivened her. She had buried the baby within her that still longed for a supportive relationship with a parent. Her personality that seemed a whirlwind of frenetic activity rested upon a weak psychic foundation.

Marilyn brutally drove herself to complete her tasks, which seemed to take all of her strength. She was obsessed with dirt and she cleaned fanatically. She was removed from other persons. If one of the family members tried to speak to her, she felt intruded upon. She could only relate to others by role-playing.

Marilyn managed to function in daily life but only with great effort. Nightly she would awaken in dread of what would become of her when she grew old, infirm, impoverished. There would be no one to take care of her. It was the helpless, terrified infantile needy self that awakened. The fear of aging was an expression of the infantile self's dread of abandonment, isolation, and helplessness. These awakenings were not comprised of rage or persecution but rather with fervent need and loneliness. She looked over at her sleeping husband and wanted to awake him but worried that he was pale and drained. He had a chronic medical condition that had been in remission but she feared she would exhaust him and make him ill.

I remarked, "You barely keep yourself going each day by entombing the baby within you that is longing to be loved. Each night, that baby awakens screaming silently for love. You look over at your husband and long to suck the love right out of him but then you are in terror that your love is destructive and will empty him of his lifeblood, leaving you utterly alone. This fear that your love is destructive must go back to your early relationship with your mother when she was physically ill (I recall she had her first stroke when you were two) and also emotionally brutalized by your father. It must have been in that relationship that you first had the sense that your need to be loved was somehow bad, destructive, greedy. Looking into your husband's pale, worn, exhausted face must have reminded you of looking into your mother's suffering visage. Every night you relive the baby longing to suck the love from your mother. When she died of the second stroke—something wrong with the blood flow—it must have confirmed your view that your love was destructive, that you somehow drained her of her lifeblood. You must at times have looked at your mother with longing but the look you found must have silently replied, 'What do you want, my blood?' "

The dissociation of the infantile need to be loved turned this natural longing into greed. A need that should have been fulfilled became the consuming core of her being, an identity tag—that of the greedy child—that she wore from the moment she awakened until she went to sleep. Thus, she had no choice but to entomb this identity component of the needy, greedy, destructive child that cried out with longing each night.

She listened to my direct interpretations with great interest, responding that they felt right, made sense, and that she needed to think more and integrate these ideas. The following week she announced that a reality problem arose that distracted her from pondering over the preceding session. The situation reported typifies dissociation serving as a resistance. The patient had an elderly aunt who was an infantile, demanding, needy, and manipulative woman, the sister of the patient's father. She was to enter a hospital for surgery the next week. This surgery had been planned well beforehand. What was new was that Marilyn wanted to be at the aunt's bedside so that she would not come out of the surgery and be alone. Originally, the aunt's immediate family had intended to be there but now her husband was too depressed over a forthcoming trial to wait at the hospital. Their adult children had made other plans.

Marilyn's wishes caused a rift with her husband. She expected him to drop his personal plans to serve as a volunteer at a community function, in order to take her to the hospital. He reluctantly agreed but complained that she was being overly helpful, which allowed the aunt's family to avoid responsibility. The original plan had been for Marilyn and her husband to visit on the day following the surgery. The husband favored this plan. Marilyn described these events in terms of her anger at her husband. This illustrates how the dissociated self can be weaved into a complicated realistic situation.

I was alerted to the possibility that this situation could be related to the previous week's insight about the dissociated, needy self. First there was the patient's announcement that the new situation had, unfortunately, nothing to do with our previous session. In addition, the crisis was not created suddenly but rather by a change that the patient made in her plans. Freud (1925) remarked that the negation of an idea often speaks of its truth. Thus the patient's statement that this new crisis had nothing to do with our significant discussion of the preceding week suggested the opposite.

I remarked that I saw at least one connection from the previous session. "During our last time together, we discussed your late-night fears of aging, which I related to the infantile self's fear of isolation and abandonment. This week you have discussed an aging aunt and your concerns that she will feel isolated and abandoned upon awakening from surgery. I am wondering whether the infantile self which was embodied in your own fear of aging is now embodied in your aging aunt?"

The patient did not immediately respond but instead discussed her feelings that it was her responsibility to her aunt, that she couldn't bear the idea of her aunt awakening alone and rage at her husband for not understanding her feelings. She wanted immediate help to determine how to insure her husband's cooperation.

I said that I was also not immediately responding to the situation. I explained that she may do what she pleased about the aunt—it was her choice—but that sometimes an analysis of the internal situation could help sort out the confusion so that one could choose with clarity. Marilyn acknowledged that while fighting with her husband about these issues, she felt it was archaic but she couldn't quite understand what was happening. She said, "I do not feel identified with my aunt."

I said, "Your sense of yourself—the I—becomes completely embodied in your helper self so long as you have your aunt to embody your infantile self. It is no accident that you have chosen your aunt for this purpose. You have spoken of her many times before as needy, greedy, and manipulative. She is the perfect container for these unacceptable aspects of your self. So long as you have your aunt to house these unwanted self components, you do not have to feel identified with infantile needs. This enables you to become completely identified with the helping function. It is an effort to achieve autonomy while, at the same time, a resistance to bringing in the needy self to me for help. You are protecting me from what you believe to be your destructive, greedy need for loving by attempting to "cure" yourself without any help. Your project to help your aunt is secretly an effort at self-cure."

In the next session, the patient reported that directly upon leaving me, she telephoned her husband and told him that he was off the hook. Next, she called her uncle and insisted that if he wants her at the hospital he must take her. He complained that he would have to go, and she said he should, it is his wife. He said he could not sit there thinking of the impending trial, and she said she would wait with him. She witnessed the truth of my remarks. When the aunt awakened from surgery she screamed for her mother. She realized how the aunt could embody Marilyn's infantile self-longing for the mother. Marilyn's son, studying to be a psychologist, observed her caring for the aunt and remarked "You are actually mothering yourself when you take care of her. This is what you had always done with me."

The Case of Ernest

This final case vignette illustrates further how the dissociated self is significant in the schizoid patient's detachment in the transferential relationship.

Ernest was a middle-aged male patient in therapy with a male therapist whom I supervised. A homosexual, Ernest lived independently and was gainfully employed in advertising. He reported that he had never experienced a satisfactory relationship with his unresponsive father, a self-absorbed man who separated permanently from the family during Ernest's latency years. If Ernest went to the father with a problem, he was made to feel weak. After the separation he felt himself an intruder in his father's presence. He grew up with his mother and sisters. He felt adrift.

In his adult life, he established relationships with dependent adolescent boys. These relationships followed a similar pattern. He would shower his lovers with love, gifts, and attention, then feel that they exploited him, used him, and were not loyal or appreciative. Ernest became depressed and needy of recognition. He sought treatment.

For nearly a year in therapy he had not felt dependence, anger, or eroticism in the transference. He experienced the therapeutic relationship as professional and had no personal feelings toward the therapist. He felt a detachment in the relationship and likened it to a box left on a shelf in his mind—compartmentalized in its place—and only attended to during the actual therapeutic hour. Meanwhile, the patterns of his relationship and life continued to disturb him but were unaffected by the treatment.

The patient decided to find "a young male hustler" from the classified ads of a gay publication. He selected someone with the name of John, which happened also to be the name of the therapist. During the next months, he complained that he had to pay the hustler for love and sex, but what he needed was to be loved unconditionally and freely.

The therapist interpreted that the patient split off his feelings of frustration and rejection in the transference relationship onto a male hustler of the same name and insinuated unconsciously that he experienced the therapist as a hustler. The patient could not see the connection. He realistically responded that the two relationships were directed toward different needs—the hustler met personal needs for love and sex even though he was a paid professional, whereas the therapist met only therapeutic strivings. The patient's statement was entirely appropriate and realistic. However Little (1986) states that schizoid patients may use the awareness of reality to defend against a delusion, especially in relation to an unconscious delusional transference. The patient's relationship to the hustler seemed to be acting out the dependency conflicts prompted by the therapeutic relationship in a split transference (Volkan 1987).

I have noted (Seinfeld 1990), "The patient's tie to an external bad object, especially if it commences or becomes intense in the course of treatment, could reflect the splitting off or displacement of a bad object (or ambivalently split transference)" (p. 219).

Interpretations of the split-object transference, usually effective in the treatment of borderline patients, often have no therapeutic effect in the treatment of schizoid patients. The dissociation makes the split-object transference uninterpretable. In other words, the "male hustler" cannot be understood as a split-off part of the therapist parental image. Instead, the patient reverses the infantile need for the parental figure. The "male hustler" represents the patient's infantile needy self that has been dissociated. The transference situation augments the need for the father figure. But the patient does not directly split off that need onto an external object. Instead, the patient identifies with the father/therapist parental image and projects the needy self into the external object, in this case the male hustler. The patient's need for the therapist is projected into the male hustler, who then is expected to direct that need to the patient himself. The need goes around full circle. The greater the patient's dependency need for the therapist, the more extensive was his need to displace the needy self into the hustler. The patient needs to be needed by the hustler with the same intensity that he needs the therapist.

The hustler has the same name as the therapist and is also paid for service. This suggests that initially, the hustler does serve as a split-off therapist parental imago, but the patient immediately inverts this situation by projecting the infantile self into the form of the hustler. Therefore, the therapist must first interpret the dissociated needy self in the external object and the patient's identification with the parental figure. It is this intervention that will then bring about an interpretable split-object transference. In other words, the patient will become aware that the hustler had initially represented the split-off need for the therapist, which was then defended against by dissociating the infantile self into the hustler. The schizoid patient actually defends against the split transference (itself a defense) through dissociation and inversion of infantile self and parental imago, and this mechanism is one of the secrets of his disengagement in the transference.

As a child, the patient longed for an available father. Unsuccessful in his efforts to achieve a good object relationship with the father, he endeavored to become the father. In this way, he projected his infantile need for a father into the dependent youths. He characterized them as exploitive, manipulative, insatiable. He perceived them in the same terms that his father perceived him. Underlying the infantile need for the object is a primary fear of annihilation based on inner emptiness (Little 1986). Thus the need for the father is felt as a life-and-death situation, as basic as the need for oxygen. It is the intensity of this need that results in a psychotic delusion of unity with the object. The patient uses reality as a defense against this delusional transference, which is acted out in the external world by the complex maneuvers described above. It is therapeutically valuable to permit the patient to speak about himself through projection. Direct interpretations of dissociated sub-selves should be based upon a strong alliance between patient and therapist.

5

ACTING OUT, ADDICTIONS, AND COMPULSIONS IN SCHIZOID STATES

Acting out in schizoid states is a reaction to the fear of engulfment. The acting out behavior may be ego syntonic, or the acting out may be dissociated from a passive compliant self.

ACTING OUT AND THE FEAR OF BEING PETRIFIED INTO AN OBJECT

Schizoid patients often find the ordinary demands of life to be affronts to their freedom. They are acutely sensitive to awakening on a schedule, smiling and having to say good morning on the job, submitting to the structure, prohibitions, and commands of the workplace. Sigmund Freud's *Civilization and Its Discontents* is often mistakenly considered a conservative or reactionary book. In actuality, Freud shows considerable empathy for the schizoid person's point of view. Freud states that civilization requires a renunciation of absolute freedom for a degree of security. Freud believes the sacrifice is necessary, but he acknowledges the trade-off and the inevitable discontent. Therefore, the schizoid individual has a piece of the truth in his sensitivity to the alienating aspects of adaptation. Ego psychology, with its emphasis on ego autonomy and the value of adaptation, may be inadvertently neglecting this truth.

The schizoid individual may perceive the ordinary rules and regulations of life as engulfments. For example, one patient automatically leaps over subway turnstiles; on seeing a No Smoking sign she lights a cigarette, or is provoked at a sign reading 55 m.p.h. to step on the gas. Schizoids may be hyperalert to such ordinances as: Enter, Exit, Go, Stop, Yield, No Left Turn, No Right Turn, Caution, No Parking. These signs are perceived as the commands of an engulfing parental object. It is not that this viewpoint is all inappropriate, but rather that the schizoid may be locked into only this one view. The acting out is a response to anxiety about being objectified.

As an example, a male patient thought it highly important to be described by all who knew him as "unpredictable." If he sensed that anyone pictured him to be kind, he would behave obnoxiously, or if someone had the idea he was obnoxious he would then appear kind. He was afraid of becoming petrified into whatever image the other had of him. Greek mythology expressed the theme that the gods could turn humans into stone. Laing (1959) states that in petrification and depersonalization the anxiety is that the live person will be transformed into a dead thing, an it, a stone, a robot, an automaton without subjectivity or autonomy.

The schizoid patient may rebel against becoming a mere object through oppositionalism, defiance, and omnipotent control. The work situation is often particularly trying because there is the danger of becoming petrified into the work role. Sartre (1956) described the task of filling a role without fully becoming it in his passage of the waiter in the cafe in *Being and Nothingness.* He describes the waiter's movements as too rapid, jaunty, and automatic. The look in his eye, the tone of voice, express an interest that is too solicitous. He carries the tray with the restlessness of a tightrope walker. He imitates the walk of an automaton. He appears to be playing a game. It becomes clear that he amuses himself, he is playing— that is, playing at being the person we call a waiter.

Atwood and Stolorow (1984) criticize Sartre, stating that Sartre does not believe an individual can fully identify with a role. I believe they are revealing a conformist, adaptive trend that self psychology has inherited from ego psychology. This issue is not merely theoretical, but very important in the clinical work with schizoids. The key word used by Sartre is "play." The work of Winnicott would suggest that the idea of playing a role but not fully becoming the role is not an indication of pathology. The problem for the schizoid patient is that he cannot "play" at the role. The role is taken too seriously; the schizoid becomes fully identified with it. One may securely play at a role and identify with it only if one is not afraid of losing oneself in it.

I recall a schizoid patient who found a job as a clerk. Immediately, he wanted to quit. He did not want to be a clerk for the rest of his life. In a state of agitation, he obsessed about various jobs he might try. He would not act the part of a clerk. Although he had not shown any great interest in art previously, he fantasized about being an artist who was working as a clerk. In this way, he could continue to function in the role of clerk. Sartre notes that a salesperson who responds to the public as an artist, and who dreams of being an artist, becomes offensive to the patrons.

There is an important distinction between the problem of schizoids and borderlines in the workplace. Both may defy work regulations, authority, and schedules. However, their motivations are often different. In acting out, the borderline typically expresses a sense of helplessness, weakness, the wish to be taken care of. He is crying, "Everyone demands too much of me. I can't do it. I'm helpless, take care of me." The schizoid patient is not expressing helplessness but rather rebels against engulfment and being petrified into an object of the workplace. The schizoid patient is often quite competent and hard-working, and, unlike the borderline patient, does not suffer from generalized ego weakness. The problem is that the schizoid often functions in opposition to the general system of the workplace. He will create his own systems, which are antisocial functions. The schizoid often disparages the established ways of doing things. Diane, a patient (Seinfeld 1990), worked at a series of jobs where she would create her own systems, which were always at odds with the general office routines. Exploration of this tendency revealed that she could not tolerate being a cog in the wheel and having to fit into a way of working that was not of her own creation. Diane's anxiety was similar to that of the patient mentioned in Chapter 2 who feared being an object in another person's dream.

The schizoid patient who fears engulfment or being petrified into an object is attempting to protect the isolated, secret self from impingement. Winnicott's views suggest that during the early formative states, these patients lacked protection from impingement by a noisy, chaotic, or unattuned environment. Winnicott (1956) stresses that the antisocial adolescent is protesting against environmental failure and the deprivation of good ego care, and that the antisocial tendency is therefore a sign of hope. In the antisocial tendency the true secret self is protected by oppositionalism. Winnicott compares the antisocial schizoid patient to the false-self passive-compliant schizoid who is hopeless and has permitted himself to be petrified and engulfed. The last chapter of this book will focus on the false-self passive-compliant schizoid patient. In a sense, the antisocial, oppositional schizoid has also established a false self in that his conduct is determined in opposition to what the other desires, and not on the basis of his own desires separate from the other. Nevertheless, there is hope and protest in the antisocial schizoid as compared to the passive-compliant patient, who desires only what the other wishes him to desire.

SCHIZOID REVOLUTION AND DICTATORSHIP

The schizoid rebels against an object. In a corrupt or failing institution, the schizoid may have the detachment and independence to identify problems that others avoid seeing, and be the first to call out, "the emperor has no clothes." Persons who are not pathologically schizoid but are subject to schizoid states may be able to selectively draw upon a schizoid detachment in certain situations and not comply with societally sanctioned destructive conduct. This individual may not join the majority who blindly follow orders to adapt to authority.

The pathologically schizoid also may be vulnerable to becoming a tyrant. This step involves assuming the position of absolute subject and transforming others into objects. This is the ultimate defense to avoid becoming an object. The revolutionary who becomes a dictator operates on this basis. There are many other tyrants in families, relationships, and work who function similarly.

TREATMENT CONSIDERATIONS

In treating the individual who is fearful of becoming objectified, the therapist must be careful that the patient does not come to believe the therapist wants the patient to conform for the therapist's sake. This belief is a pitfall and results in the patient becoming more oppositional. These patients may have had parents who wanted them to succeed in life for the parents' sake. It is concluded that anything accomplished will be stolen by the parent. The schizoid protects the possibility of future accomplishments by not accomplishing anything. Hence nothing can be stolen.

One patient lost ten jobs in the course of a little more than a year. She either quit or was fired. She repeatedly expected me to feel disappointed, frustrated, angry, or hopeless. My only comment was "How was it for you, losing the job?" I emphasized the *for you*. Sometimes, she would announce in a challenging tone that she was fired. I asked how that felt. She answered sarcastically, "How do you think it was?" I stated that I did not know. She might feel badly about the loss of money, her feelings might be hurt, she might feel it was unjustified or justified. She might feel good, she might plan to go to the beach, she might think she will get a better job. She might think she'll never work again. I responded to emphasize that my interest was in how the job affected her and that I did not have a preestablished notion of how it affected her. This intervention was directed toward her anxiety about being an object. I mentioned all of the possibilities in order to emphasize her subjectivity, that there was no one way to feel or respond. I did not immediately express empathy by insinuating how badly she must feel, nor did I offer interpretations concerning fear of independence or engulfment.

After a time, she remarked that I never seemed disappointed, and that I was different from her parents, who acted as if they were the ones losing the job. Later, she spontaneously complained that losing all of these jobs was costly. She finally indicated that she would endeavor to keep a job but then lose it. She then expressed a wish to understand why she lost jobs. She wondered whether she was in some way responsible, even though she hadn't the faintest idea of what she might have done. It was only at this point that I began to directly interpret her fear of becoming objectified and engulfed. Once I began to interpret, I did so actively and regularly.

ADDICTIONS AND COMPULSIONS

Schizoids frequently act out with substance and alcohol abuse and other addictions. Addictions serve as substitutes for human relationships. A drug abuser said: "Drugs are better than people. When I need them, they are always there. I just need the money to buy them. People are unreliable. Drugs don't disappoint you, leave you, talk back to you or rob you. Drugs have no mind or will of their own. I recommend drugs over people any day."

This patient reflects the British object relational view on drug abuse. The substitute of a nonhuman for a human object is the schizoid defense. The drug represents the internal exciting object. It presents the illusion that it is completely subject to human control. Thus, it fits the purpose of internalization, to convert the I–thou relationship into an I–it relationship. However, like the internal exciting object, the drug eludes the patient's control. It excites further need and is only temporarily satisfying. The addict often refers to it as "she." One addict called heroin his "soothing white pet." Another referred to crack as his "bad mama." I knew a female addict who termed crack her "boyfriend." Not all addicts name their drug, but there often is the trace of a personal feeling about the relationship.

Drug addiction is the perfect intersection for schizoid and symbiotic experience. Drug addicts increasingly need other persons only as a means to the drug. The addiction enables them not to need people for themselves. Addicts are frequently non-relating. At the same time, the soothing effect of the drug provides the sense of a symbiotic union. Some drugs also provide stimulation and excitement. The object relations view emphasizes that the drug use and alcoholism reinforce the fantasy of union with an internal object, while enabling the addict to be indifferent to the external object world. Addiction is therefore schizoid and symbiotic.

A middle-aged female patient with three adolescent children had been a heavy drinker for twenty years. She was employed full-time as a cocktail waitress. She was always engaged in frantic activity, rushing through her job, socializing with friends after hours, racing to do her shopping and laundering. She tried to stop drinking twice but shortly afterward started smoking pot, which led again to drinking.

She finally stopped drinking after a stroke. She came for treatment while she was recovering from the stroke. She also became involved with Alcoholics Anonymous. As she resumed the tasks of shopping, laundering, walking her dog, and so on, she felt overwhelmed with anxiety. She wondered how in the past she did these chores so easily and felt the alcohol probably fueled her and permitted her to do everything frantically. She criticized herself now for not doing enough and pushed herself to do more. I tried to slow her down, encouraging her to do no more than she was ready, and to ask her family to help. She was responsive to my suggestions, took her time in resuming her functions, and was able to do so at her own pace. She sometimes felt guilty about lying in bed with the TV and feeling cozy beneath the covers, but I encouraged her to comfort herself. It has been ten years now and she remains alcohol-free.

She credits the stroke with enabling her to stop drinking. She said that she experienced the stroke as a rebirth. The stroke allowed her to express dependency needs and be mothered by those around her. When she returned home her house was transformed into a hospital while her mother, adolescent children, friends, and relatives continued to nurse her. The recovery permitted her to fulfill her dependency needs in a therapeutic regression. My function in the treatment was one of management in terms of helping the family and patient to create a holding environment. Her parental introjects had always demanded that she should be on the go, doing and behaving frantically, never admitting that she needed help or was vulnerable. Thus, she directed all of her dependency needs toward alcohol, which was a pseudo-grown-up way to give herself "the bottle." Physical illness allowed her to express her dependency needs directly, not through alcohol, because physical illness was a socially acceptable reason to accept dependence and as it was also more acceptable to her negative introjects. Even so, during the treatment and management of the case, on occasion I had to address the concerns and resistances of the introjects and the environment.

The therapeutic regression lessened her need to drink and permitted her to resume "doing" based on a self more deeply rooted in "being." Winnicott (1963) states that the oral, greedy needs may sometimes serve the false self in terms of compensating for a failure in the fulfillment of the true self's need for primary love. The patient's alcoholism was the expression of this active orally, greedy false self, which finally receded when the true self was allowed expression.

Addictions may not be only to drugs and alcohol. Individuals may also be addicted to nonhuman objects. A patient said he was addicted to his computer. The computer was perfectly responsive. He said it only gives back what you put in. It seems to be a cross between the human and the nonhuman. The patient named it Betsy, petted it for luck, and talked to it endearingly. At the same time, he was aware that he was addicted to it precisely because it has no will of its own and is perfectly responsive to his programming. In Winnicott's terms, the computer seems to serve a transitional object function (1951). The patient talks about the computer incessantly in the therapy. Because the addiction is not self-destructive in the way that heroin or crack is, the therapist permits the patient to relate to him solely through the focus upon the transitional object.

It is possible to be addicted to sex, love, money, food, clothes, and the like. One female patient resembled the lead character in the film *Looking for Mr. Goodbar*. She was a nurturing, rather prim and proper special-education teacher. At night, she desperately sought out men for brief sexual contacts. Typically, she would meet a man in a bar, go into one of the public bathrooms, and perform fellatio upon him. She had no interest in ever meeting the man again but was addicted to this activity. It is likely that the children she taught represented her dissociated infantile self, hungry for love. She vicariously loved herself through showering her love on the children. She remained exclusively identified with the parental giving function. Each night, her needy self emerged, starving for love but expressed through the need for sex. One wonders whether either fantasized or real incest in the family of origin became the way of making contact.

Trying to Fill the Empty Core

The drug or alcohol abuser is trying to fill the empty core in an effort to achieve complete and total fulfillment. Having the substance at one's disposal eliminates all need. It is the depth of the void that is responsible for the addict's desperate efforts to achieve a state of total completion. The empty hunger is too consuming to tolerate. The addicts attempt to fill the inner void of failed object relations.

The addiction also serves to provide the abuser with an identification tag. Being an alcoholic or drug addict is an all-consuming way of life; it provides him with a culture, language, and identity.

The Irresistible Impulse

I consulted about addictions and personality disorders on the substance abuse unit of a hospital. The staff used a disease/

biological model and found that their work with some of the cases was not successful. A number of the patients seemed to have personality disorders. When they gave up the drug, they would then substitute `another compulsion and eventually return to the drug. The view that these individuals had a disease that they needed to control seemed to work in the opposite way than anticipated. A fair number of the patients felt that since they had a disease, it was not under their control, no matter how hard they would try to overcome it. The staff was becoming disillusioned with this model because it seemed to fit in with the patients' addictive behavior.

The case presented was a middle-aged male adult, a long-term heroin addict. He had quit drugs a number of times but then substituted another compulsive activity. He had turned to gambling and then to an obsessive relationship with a woman. Faced with the threat of loss of his money or the woman, he returned to drugs. The patient's need for the use of the drug was an irresistible impulse. He described it as "perched upon his shoulder." The patient had been treated at the hospital at different intervals. Some of his previous therapists were present at this meeting. The therapeutic approach had always been to strengthen his conscious resolve to remain drug-free, to strengthen his impulse control, judgment, and frustration tolerance. He was told that he had a lifetime disease that he must resist. There would be an alliance formed between the patient and the therapist. For a time, there was a cooperative, motivated determination and resolve. Unfortunately, at some point an overwhelming impulse arose like a tidal wave and entirely submerged the patient's resolve.

THE THEORY OF DYNAMIC STRUCTURE

Classical psychoanalytic theory and biological determinism shared a nineteenth-century outlook on the theory of impulse and structure. Both views hold that there is a divorce between

energy and structure. Energy acts as a pure impulse and
activates inert, pure structure from the outside. The pure
impulse, genetically based according to the biological model
and instinctually in the classical model, activates an inert
passive structure. These theories are reflected in this patient's
description of his addiction. The impulse is perched upon his
shoulder, tempting him. Thus, there is a division between
impulse and structure. The impulse is perceived as outside of
him, tempting him. He is separate from the impulse, passive.
It acts upon him with a life of its own. Fairbairn (1946)
challenged the biological determinist model. He claimed that
it was based upon an outmoded theory of physics. The idea
that energy and structure are divorced is based upon the
Helmholtzian mechanical model of the universe. Structure is
described as solid balls of atoms equivalent to billiard balls
that are activated by a separate force of energy. Basing his
views on modern physics, Fairbairn contended that structure
and energy are indivisible. The impulse is no more than the
activity of the structure.

The implication of this view has direct clinical relevance.
It challenges the notion that a pure impulse acts on a passive
self. The impulse itself must be the activity or the expression
of a self state. It is felt as coming from outside the self and as
pure impulse because the self state it belongs to is dissociated.
Pure impulses are communications from a self state dissociated from the central self. Theories based on the divorce of
impulse and structure are reinforcing the pathological dissociation. Fairbairn's view suggests that the pure impulse for
drugs is the expression of a dissociated self state that was
originally hungry for human love. As the need for dependence
was unacceptable and pushed out of consciousness, it returned
as an irresistible, senseless impulse.

Fairbairn's theory challenges the conception of an id that
is a separate reservoir of instinctual energy activating a passive, inert ego structure. Instead, he suggests that the id is

comprised of an active self state, the libidinal ego attached to an exciting object. It is this dependent object relationship that becomes expressed as a pure impulse in a state of dissociation. It is the anti-libidinal ego (or self) that is responsible for the dissociation, and this, along with the ideal object, later becomes the superego. The central ego later becomes synonymous with Freud's ego. I would suggest that on the metapsychological, purely theoretical level, it does not matter if one retains the Freudian id, ego, or superego as metaphors of the mind. However, on a clinical level, it is imperative to view the pure impulse as the action of a dissociated self. Energy and structure cannot be separated clinically.

Treatment Implications

If the therapist endeavors only to strengthen the ego against the irresistible impulse, he will strengthen dissociation, thereby guaranteeing that the impulse will increase in power, given that it remains separate from and uninfluenced by the remaining personality. The therapist working with drug abusers is often afraid to allow the patient to express or permit the need for the drug. There is often the attitude that the impulse must be held at bay, like a savage, hungry dog, at all costs. This is an error. This increases the power of the impulse.

The alliance must be formed with the part of the patient who wants to be drug-free, and at the same time reach the secret, dissociated self that is starved and filling itself with drugs. When the patient says that the impulse is like something perched on his shoulder, tempting him into drugs, the therapist should respond that the impulse is from a part of himself that he has rejected. It sits on his shoulder because he puts it there as a part of himself seated there. Having no voice, it can only be expressed as pure need. The therapist must also empathize with that part of the individual that resists the impulse, that is fearful of being overwhelmed and endeavors to get along in the world by renouncing all need. That part of the patient needs to hear that the therapist wants to bring the hungry self back into the patient, not to submerge his will, but to strengthen his influence over the entire personality. The implication is that when a recently drug- or alcohol-free patient talks only about his determined motivation to remain clean he may be heading for trouble. The therapist must reach out for the silent voice of need. Furthermore, it is erroneous to believe the addict can make a resolution never to abuse drugs and realistically follow through. It is only one self state that has made the resolution. Also, because of his fear of engulfment, he will begin to feel trapped by his resolution. The choice to be drug- or alcohol-free must always be active. The patient chooses to be drug-free every day. The therapist stresses that the patient must always be actively making a choice. The therapist is not neutral. He tells the patient that he wants to see the hungry, needy self receive the help and care it needs. The therapist is quite direct that drugs are not the solution. But it is also emphasized that it is ultimately the patient's choice and that the therapist wants him to solve his problems for *himself,* not because the therapist wishes to dominate him. These ideas need to be stated explicitly because the schizoid addict does not take them for granted.

I believe organizations such as Alcoholics Anonymous, Pills Anonymous, and the like are sometimes extremely helpful to substance abusers, providing them a forum for human dependence as a substitute for the chemical dependence. Alcoholics Anonymous offers a sponsor available 24 hours daily. These organizations strive to reach the dissociated infant that is hungry but fearful of human contact.

The Divorce between Thought and Action

Schizoid patients express the split between thought and action. In inner-city agencies it is not uncommon for patients to profess the desire for treatment but then not to keep appointments. Often they have disorganized, chaotic lives and multiple problems. Frequent missed appointments prompt the therapist to believe that the patient is allowing outside circumstances to interfere with their therapy. When the therapist raises the issue of resistance, the patient typically insists that he has no ambivalence and is firm about wanting the treatment. This type of patient is not lying. He is conscious only of wanting the help. He is almost pathologically one-minded. He has no awareness he might not want the help on another level. I suggest that the part of the patient that does not want to come is not expressed in thought but expressed through action. He expresses the wish not to come by not coming, while thinking he wants to come. The action is a communication of the dissociated self. The action aborts the thought. These patients typically dissociate in most areas of living. A patient I discussed earlier, Diane, displayed massive dissociation. She was once desperate to go on a job interview, but arriving in Manhattan by subway, she walked in the wrong direction and missed the opportunity.

Direct Interpretation

The therapist may effectively intervene with direct interpretation. First, it is necessary for the therapist to acknowledge explicitly that he does not believe the patient lied or acted purposively. This sets the stage for intervention. The therapist may then say, "I know that you consciously were one-minded about coming. I know that you made every conscious effort to come. Sometimes we may think we want something, but our actions may suggest that we may want something other than what we think we want. Did you ever hear the phrase 'actions speak louder than words'? It is this idea, that action speaks, that I am trying to convey. Action sometimes speaks of unconscious feelings. By your not coming, you may have been talking with your feet. Consciously you may want to come but unconsciously another part of you may not want to come. Are you aware that it is not unusual for a person to feel two ways about coming here? It is like Hamlet—to come or not to come. I have this sense that you are a person who genuinely tries to do what you think is the right thing. Feelings that go against the right thing never enter your mind. But those feelings demand expression, and they communicate by action."

Direct interpretations are often wordy and long, but for many schizoid patients they serve the need for feedback and provide a nonthreatening method of feeding the infantile self. Thus, these interventions have a relational aspect as well as an insightful one.

THE EATING DISORDERS: THE BODY
AS A METAPHOR OF SCHIZOID STATES

The schizoid's endeavor to achieve psychic emptiness or complete fulfillment are most clearly expressed in the eating disorders of anorexia and bulimia. In binge eating, the schizoid tries to achieve a state of absolute fullness. Anorexia is the ultimate attempt to repress and dissociate the infantile, needy, hungry self. The body becomes a metaphor for the empty core. The anorexic aspires to the ideal of emptiness. It is the hunger of the need for love, the empty core, that the individual attempts to fill with food. Anorexia is then a reaction to the insatiable need for fulfillment. The earliest experience that the infant shares with the primary caregiver centers around food. Eating is therefore the first social experience. The individual's attitude toward food may reflect his attitude toward the primary caregiver. The schizoid individual may substitute food for the human object just as the drug addict substitutes chemical dependence for human dependence. Infantile dependency conflicts become transformed into issues of taking in, expelling, or avoiding food. In this sense, the eating disorder may be reflective of an underlying schizoid condition. The individual starving himself thereby becomes obsessed with food. There is no better way to make oneself feel that one needs nothing other than food than to starve. It guarantees one shall think of nothing but food every waking moment.

6

THE TRAGIC CASE
OF ELLEN WEST

Binswanger wished to illustrate his views on existential analysis through a case history. Binswanger went back into the archives in the sanitorium of which he was the director to select the case of Ellen West, who had eventually committed suicide. The case history was comprised of a wealth of material, including Ellen West's diaries, personal notes, and poetry, the summaries of two treatments by psychoanalysts before her admission to the sanitorium, and diagnostic consultations while in the sanitorium by Bleuler and Kraepelin. Binswanger used the case as a basis for viewing how Ellen West was diagnosed and understood by the two psychoanalysts, and then by Bleuler and Kraepelin and the authorities of the clinic, compared to how he finally understood her on the basis of existential analysis twenty-six years later. Binswanger applied Heidegger's (1927) concept of *Dasein,* human existence or being, to a specific human existence or individuality, which he referred to as "Dasein analysis." Thus, Binswanger stated that the case history pertains to a "human individuality" named Ellen West.

Binswanger was born in Switzerland, in 1881, into a family of physicians. He completed his medical studies in Zurich and was recommended by Freud to become a member of the Vienna Psychoanalytic Society when the Zurich group, under Jung, split from the International Society. Binswanger joined the Vienna Society in 1907 and was analyzed by Freud. Binswanger became increasingly critical of the diagnostic, scientific, and medical outlook of psychoanalysis, as he increasingly favored understanding the patient existentially in accord with Heidegger's analysis of human existence. May (1983) states that although Binswanger radically differed from Freud's views, he nevertheless remained Freud's friend, and their personal relationship survived their differences. He remarks that the friendship between Binswanger and Freud was the only occasion of Freud's continuing a relationship with a colleague who had differed radically with him.

Ellen West came to the sanatorium in 1918, when Binswanger was 37 years old and psychoanalysis was still being formulated. Schoenewolf (1990a) states that Binswanger was 63 when he published the case and that he used it to contrast the crude methods of the period of Ellen West's treatment with the way Ellen West would have been understood by the advances in existential analysis. During her long illness, her condition was diagnosed as schizophrenia, obsessional neurosis, constitutional psychopathy and manic–depression. Today, she would be diagnosed as having severe anorexia nervosa. The case history illustrates nearly all of the schizoid phenomena discussed in this volume.

> Ellen West was the only daughter of a father "for whom her love and veneration knew no bounds" (Binswanger 1944). The father was a formal, reserved, willful man of action who suffered from self-reproaches, states of fear, and nocturnal depressions. Mother was a suggestible, anxious, soft and kindly woman who experienced a three-year depression during the period of her engagement. The mother's father died

young but the mother's mother was manic-depressive and came from a family in which there were "many psychotics" (p. 238). The father's sister became mentally ill on his wedding day, and of the father's brothers, one shot himself, another committed suicide, two fell ill of dementia arteriosclerosis and died of strokes, and the fifth was eccentric. Ellen had a brother four years older that she described as healthy and well adjusted, and a younger brother who was admitted to a psychiatric clinic because of suicidal tendencies.

Ellen was said to have experienced a normal birth. At nine months, she reportedly refused milk and was therefore fed meat broth. In later years, she remained unwilling to tolerate milk. She liked meat but rejected vegetables and desserts. However, Binswanger states, as Ellen herself later confessed, she was not averse to sweets but rather loved them and rejected them in an early act of renunciation. If food was forced on her, she strongly resisted it. During two periods of psychoanalytic treatment in later life, she reported few memories about her early years and little was known about her childhood. According to the statements of her parents and her own memories, she was a defiant, violently headstrong child. She would defy an order of her parents for hours and even then did not carry it out. In one incident someone showed her a bird's nest but she denied it was one and stubbornly held to her own view. Even during her childhood, she was depressed and the world seemed empty and bleak.

At the age of 10 she moved with her family to Europe, where she went to a school for girls. Binswanger did not identify her original homeland. She was an excellent student, liked school, and was very ambitious. She would never miss school even if she was ill and the doctor ordered it, fearing she might fall behind. She would weep for hours if she did not rank first in her favorite subjects—history and German. She was strong-willed and chose the motto: *Aut Caesar Aut Nihil* (either Caesar or Nothing)! She was said to be "boyish" and preferred to wear trousers in situations where it was considered highly inappropriate. She was a thumb-sucker from her infancy, but at 16 she suddenly gave it up along with her boyish games at the onset of an infatuation which lasted two years. But in a poem written in her 17th year, she continued to express the ardent desire to be a boy, to be a soldier, to fear no foe, and to joyously die, sword in hand.

Her other poetry during this time showed a marked variability of mood. One poem sings that her heart beats with exultant joy, now the sky is darkened, the winds blew weirdly, and the ship of her life sails on unguided, not knowing whither to direct its keel. In another poem the wind rushes about her ears, she longs for it to cool her burning brow; she runs against it blindly as if stepping out of a confining tomb, as if flying through the air in an uncontrollable urge to freedom; she must achieve something great but then her gaze falls back onto the world again and a saying comes to her mind "Man, in small things make your world." She cries, "Fight on" (p. 239).

During this time of her life she was occupied with social problems, feeling deeply the contrast between her own privileged social position and that of the masses, and drawing up plans to improve their lot. She read extensively and was influenced by a popular Scandinavian novel, Niels Lyhne, about a disillusioned idealist, and her convictions changed from deep religiosity to atheism.

In her diary entries from her 18th year, she praises the blessings of work. She wonders, "What would we be without work, what would become of us," and says that they would have to enlarge cemeteries for those who would go to death by their own hand. "When all the joints of the world threaten to fall apart, when the light of our happiness is extinguished and our pleasure in life lies wilting, only one thing saves us from madness 'work.' Then we throw ourselves into a sea of duties as into Lethe and the roar of its waves is to drown out the death-knell pealing in our heart" (p. 240).

In that same year (her 18th), she was enthusiastic about a trip to Paris with her parents. However, even the poems during this trip continued to show her contradictory moods. One poem sings of sunshine, the smiling spring, the radiant skies over the free, wide, vast land of bliss and pleasure, but in another poem the only longing left to her is that of darkness, death, and morbidity.

A journey across the ocean with her parents when she was 19 lifted her mood. This journey lives in her recollection as "the happiest and most harmless time" of her life. She wrote in her diary of floods of light resting on villages, valleys, and grain fields with only the mountains hidden in darkness. However, on this trip, Ellen was never able to be alone—away from her parents. Later that year when she returned to Europe, she cultivated horseback riding, but with excessive intensity, trying feats that were dangerous, and vying with experienced riders in competition. Her 20th year is described as full of hopes, yearning, and happiness. Her poems sing of "the wild ecstasy of life, youthful zest bursting her breast asunder and wondering how one could lag behind and lock oneself in the 'tomb of a house' " (p. 241). She longs for her ideal lover. If he would come, no sacrifice would be too great. She requires that he should be strong, tall, a soul as pure as the morning light. He must live life and not play or dream it. She will give him all of her love and strength but he must be able to be happy, to take joy in the sunshine and warmth, to enjoy her (p. 202).

In her 20th year, she took another trip abroad and became engaged to a "romantic foreigner" but broke off the engagement at her father's wish. On the return trip, she stopped in Italy and wrote an essay, "On the woman's calling." She writes that she loves life passionately, the world belongs to her, she has the sun, wind, and beauty to herself, that she is filled with a consuming longing to learn and has had a glimpse of the secret of the universe (p. 241). These first weeks in Sicily were the last of her happiness in life. The diary again reported the shadows of dread and doubt. She reproached herself for all of the fine ideas, plans, and hopes she had written in her diary because they remained mere words instead of becoming transformed into deeds. She felt herself to be small, helpless, and utterly forsaken in a world that cannot understand her. Along with her depression emerged a new and definite dread— namely the fear of becoming fat. At the beginning of her trip to Sicily, Ellen displayed a strong appetite. Consequently, she

became fat, and her girlfriends teased her. At once, she morti-
fied herself with immoderate hikes and fasts. During a walk
her friends would stop to view a pretty scene, but Ellen
continually circled around them. She stopped eating sweets or
anything fattening and skipped meals altogether.

At 21, when she returned from Italy, she was markedly
depressed. Ellen was constantly tormented by the idea that she
was getting fat. In her diary, she complained that she was not
at home anywhere, not even with her family, that she had no
peace, could not find any satisfactory activity; that she was
constantly tortured, and that every nerve in her body quiv-
ered. She despised herself and felt at the lowest rung of the
ladder. In a poem, distress grimly sits at a grave, pale and
motionless, staring, neither flinching nor budging. The birds
and the flowers wilt and die. Death no longer appears to her as
terrible. Death is not a man with a scythe but a "glorious
woman, white asters in her dark hair, large eyes, dream-deep
and grey" (p. 242). The only thing to lure her is dying. She
longs for death, considering it the greatest happiness in life,
without which life would be unbearable.

In the fall of the same year, Ellen started to come out of
her depression. But along with an urge to act and a newly
awakened enthusiasm toward life, her paralyzing despair continued. In her diary she wrote of wanting to free herself from
the iron chains of commonplace life, convention, property,
comfort, gratitude, consideration, and strongest of all, the
unyielding chains of love. She began to write about revolution. "Do you actually preach making concessions. I will make
no concessions. You realize that the existing social order is
rotten, rotten down to the root, dirty and mean" (p. 243). She
complains that she is 21 years old but expected to be silent and
grinning like a puppet. She is no puppet, but a human being
with red blood, and a woman, with a quivering vital heart. She
cannot breathe in an atmosphere of hypocrisy and cowardice.
She longs to do something great, to get closer to her ideal. Will
it cost tears, struggle, pain? Ellen writes "Oh, what shall I do,
how shall I manage it? It boils and pounds in me, it wants to
burst the outer shell! Freedom! Revolution!—No, no, I am not

talking claptrap. I am not thinking liberation of the soul; I mean the real, tangible liberation of the people from the chains of their oppressors. Shall I express it more clearly? I want a revolution, a great uprising to spread over the entire world and overthrow the whole social order. I should like to forsake house and parents like a Russian nihilist, to live among the poorest of the poor, and make propaganda for the great cause" (pp. 243–244). During the winter, Ellen began to work on a favorite project, the Children's Reading Rooms, which she saw during her trip to America. But by the ensuing spring, the project no longer satisfied her.

In the fall of her 23rd year, she broke down after an unpleasant affair with a riding teacher. The dread of becoming fat began to be accompanied by an intensified longing for food. Eating afforded her no satisfaction in the presence of others although she enjoyed it when alone. She passed an examination in order to audit courses at the university. She entered into a love relationship with a student and they became engaged. She became enthusiastic about studying and student life. She went with friends on long hikes to the mountains and started to gain weight. She still could not be alone and always kept her old governess with her. Her parents demanded a temporary separation from her boyfriend, so she went to a seaside resort, where she suffered from severe depression. Throughout the next year she again starved herself, took long hikes without rest, and swallowed up to forty-eight thyroid tablets a day.

In her 25th year, she took her third trip overseas, where she was diagnosed as having Graves' disease, a condition of exophthalmic hypothyroid goiter. She had several weeks of bed rest and recovery, during which time she gained weight and mourned her fate. Upon her return home, she broke off the engagement to the student. In May she went to a public sanitorium, and in the summer she attended a gardening school. She lost interest in gardening and left the school prematurely. Again, she was losing weight by exhausting physical activity and scanty eating. In the fall, a cousin whom she had been friends with for many years, expressed a romantic interest in her. The broken engagement with the student remained an open wound, but she nevertheless developed a love relationship with the cousin, and they planned to marry. For two years she vacillated between her cousin and the student, with whom she resumed her relationship. She married her cousin at the age of 28. She weighed 160 pounds at her wedding, but started dieting on the honeymoon trip and rapidly lost weight. In the summer following the wedding, her menstruation ceased. She was torn between the desire for a child and the dread of becoming fat. At the time of her 29th birthday, in the autumn, she had a severe hemorrhage during a hike with her husband. Despite the hemorrhage, she continued to hike for several hours. A physician performed a curettage and discovered that she had suffered a miscarriage.

In her 30th year, she became intensely interested and involved in social work. She took genuine interest in the people committed to her care and developed personal relationships with them that sometimes kept up for years. She systematically impoverished her diet and gradually became a vegetarian. She took laxatives to keep her weight down and by the age of 32 had increased her dosage to sixty or seventy tablets a night, causing violent diarrhea and tortured vomiting. She often went outside in feverish and chilled states in hopes of developing pneumonia. She tried to occupy herself with work, exchanging her volunteer work in the welfare agency for a paid social work position. She further impoverished her diet, her weight dropping to 103 pounds. She was preoccupied with calorie charts, recipes, and so on. She spent every free moment writing recipes of delicious delectable dishes, puddings, desserts, and sweets in her cookbook. She demanded that everyone around her eat much and well, while denying everything to herself. She filled her plate like everyone else but emptied the greater part of the food into her handbag, developing great skill in hiding the fact that she hardly ate anything. She ate foods she believed to be nonfattening with great greed and haste. At times, she would eat items she bought for the household and then reproach herself severely. Her physical condition deteriorated further until she thinned down to a skeleton weighing only 92 pounds.

At the age of 32½ she underwent her first analysis, with a young and sensitive analyst. The analyst told her that her main goal was the "subjugation of all other people" (p. 250), an interpretation she believed to be "marvelously correct." During her analysis, Ellen continued to cut down on her eating. With the feelings of dread becoming more frequent, there appeared the obsession of constantly thinking of food. She soon tired of the analysis, which was terminated for external reasons. Ellen attempted suicide twice later that year, taking twenty tablets of a barbituate compound and fifty-six tablets of somnacetin, most of which, however, she vomited during the night. She started treatment with a second analyst, who viewed her as having a "father complex" and described her eating problem as "anal erotic," equating eating with becoming pregnant. Eating = being fertilized = pregnant = getting fat (p. 260). The "father complex" was manifested in the transference when she suddenly sat down on the analyst's lap to give him a kiss, and on another occasion when she wished to lay her head on his shoulder and have him call her "Ellen child" (p. 260). Before entering the sanatorium, she was diagnosed by Kraepelin as having melancholia, and her body weight had fallen to 102 pounds.

On January 14, 1918, she arrived at Binswanger's Kreuzlingen Sanatorium, where she remained with her husband until March 30, 1918. She saw Binswanger daily. She continued to take laxatives and complained that all she wanted was to be left alone to die. She dreamed vividly about food and death. She dreamed war broke out and that she was going to the field, joyous that she would soon die and glad that she could eat everything now. She dreamed that she was the wife of a painter who could not sell his paintings. She pleaded with him to get a revolver and shoot both of them since their life had become hopeless. In another dream, on a trip overseas she jumped into the water through a porthole. In the fourth dream she ordered goulash but only wanted a small portion; she complained to her old nursemaid that people torture her and she wants to set fire to herself in the forest.

On one occasion she offered fifty thousand francs to a farmer if he would shoot her quickly. She accused the doctors of being sadists who took pleasure in tormenting her, and she asked the doctors for permission to kill herself. She attempted obstinately to convince the doctor and her husband of the correctness of this idea and rejected all counterargument. Her husband gathered information on the theme of suicide for Binswanger, who was struck by her powerful wish to die. The wish to die had permeated her entire life. As a child, she thought it "interesting" to have a fatal accident—falling through the ice while skating, for instance. During her riding, she performed foolhardy tricks, had a fall in which she broke her clavicle, and was disappointed that the accident was not fatal. On the very next day, she mounted her horse and carried on in the same way. As a young girl, she was disappointed whenever a fever subsided and she recovered from illness. While taking lessons with a tutor, she was fascinated by the phrase "Those whom the Gods love die young" (p. 265) and demanded the teacher continually repeat this statement. While working in a foundling hospital, she visited children with scarlet fever and kissed them, in the hope that she would catch it. Later, with a fever of 102 degrees, she stood naked on a balcony after taking a hot bath and put her feet in ice-cold water.

She repeatedly demanded that she be discharged from the sanatorium so that she could commit suicide. She expressed the sense that a ghost was stalking her in order to kill her, and she wrote in her diary of awaiting the coming of insanity which would hurl her into the yawning abyss. Binswanger could only conceive of two options: she could either be placed in a locked ward or released into her husband's custody. Her husband wondered if there was any chance of cure. Binswanger shook his head and also informed the husband that if she were released, it was very likely that she would commit suicide. Binswanger suggested that they call in two other experts to get further opinions.

On March 24, a consultation was arranged with Professor E. Bleuler and an unnamed foreign psychiatrist. Bleuler diagnosed her as schizophrenic, while the other psychiatrist believed that she was having a "progressive unfolding of a psychopathic constitution." Both psychiatrists fully agreed with Binswanger's prognosis and opinion that there was no reliable therapy available for Ellen West. They resolved to give in to Ellen's request for a discharge.

On her return, Ellen remained distressed over her inability to deal with life. She arrived home weighing approximately 104 pounds, the same as when she was admitted. For the first two days after her discharge, she fasted, exercised, and took laxatives. On the third day, she was transformed. At breakfast she ate butter and sugar; at lunch she ate so much that she was satisfied for the first time in thirteen years. At afternoon coffee, she ate chocolate Easter eggs. She took a walk with her husband and read poems by Rilke, Storm, Goethe, and Tennyson and was amused by the first chapter of Mark Twain's *Christian Science,* saying she was in a positively festive mood. She wrote letters, the last one to a patient to whom she had become attached. That evening she took a lethal dose of poison and on the following morning she was dead. It was reported that "she looked as she had never looked in life—calm and happy and peaceful" (p. 267).

Binswanger presents an existential analysis, attempting to leave out, so far as possible, all moral, esthetic, social, and medical judgments in order to avoid prejudice and to study the modes of existence of this particular individuality who was given the name Ellen West. He rejects all use of labels and develops the concept of modes of existence from Martin Heidegger's philosophy of modes of being-in-the-world, which describes various modes of organizing experience.

Existential analysis distinguishes three modes of world, that is, "three aspects of world," characterizing each individual as being-in-the-world. The first, Umwelt, means "world around" and includes biological needs, instinctual drives, natural desires; and laws and cycles, including sleep and awakeness, life and death, desire and satisfaction. All organisms have Umwelt and are capable of being-in-the-world in the mode of Umwelt, the world without self-reflection. The second mode, Mitwelt, or "with world," is the world of interrelationships with human beings. The Mitwelt does not refer to the group as a whole, the human herd, or a collective, but rather refers to the community of individual human beings. It is the meaning that the individual gives to the group or to relationships. The third mode, Eigenwelt, means "own world" and refers to what things mean to oneself subjectively and what one makes of the world. An example of Eigenwelt is for one to experience that "this flower is beautiful for me." The individual has something to do with the beauty of the flower and creates it as beautiful for himself by his enjoyment of it. The flower is not beautiful in itself but rather for human consciousness. If no human were to even see the flower, it would exist, but not as ugly or beautiful. Beauty is what humans *make* of it and it is this capacity to make something of the world that is referred to as Eigenwelt.

Binswanger interprets Ellen West's stubbornness regarding eating, beginning at nine months, as a sign of her separation from the Umwelt—her natural biological needs. She lives in opposition to her natural biological nature. She is also in opposition to the Mitwelt—the community of humans—and closed to its influence. For instance, her negative judgment about the bird nest, "This bird nest is not bird nest" (p. 270) stands in opposition to the Mitwelt, rejecting the common perception of her human community. Binswanger asserts that the Eigenwelt (own world–self) does not go over trustingly into the Umwelt or Mitwelt to allow itself to be nurtured, supported, or fulfilled, but rather sharply opposes both the biological and social needs. Her oppositionalism results in the sense that "everything is empty" (p. 270). Her Eigenwelt is characterized by defiance and willfullness and is therefore not autonomous or authentic since it is defined by its oppositionalism, and is therefore the expression of a noninde-pendent, unauthentic, and unfree self (p. 271). Ellen's rebel-lion also extends to the "world of fate" in that she renounced her femaleness and wished to be a boy, a soldier, and played at what she considered to be only boys' games. In her Eigenwelt, she developed a certain self-sufficiency, aggressiveness, and expansiveness, based upon the denial of her Umwelt, Mit-welt, and world of fate.

Binswanger states that Ellen's work in social services and her creative interests, which lasted nearly to the end of her life, reflected her efforts to stand with both feet on the ground, to develop a practical down-to-earth self. Ellen's efforts at prac-tical action through work were not crowned with lasting success. Rather, they were opposed by Ellen's urge for aerial flight, reflected in her starvation and desperate urge toward freedom. For Ellen, walking was replaced by horseback riding in which no horse was too dangerous. Her blood rushed and soared through her arteries, every fiber trembling, her strong young body stretching itself—sitting still became impossible. Her fasting was an urge toward weightlessness, flight, the defiance of gravity. Binswanger describes her aerial, fasting world-design in her experience of riding in the sunshine, budding spring, radiant skies over the vast, wild mobile, warm, colorful earth. Ellen was attempting to escape from hunger and greed, which weighed her down beneath the earth into a swamp or tomb, an imprisoning, earthbound, decayed existence. The desire for food grew to a burdening pressure, a frantic greed that became animalization, vegetation, bestial greed. The desire to be thin was a wish for aerial flight, an urge toward freedom from the compulsion of hunger and greed.

Binswanger states, "In covertly watching Ellen while she eats, one observes that she actually throws herself on the food 'like an animal' and gobbles it down like an animal" (p. 291). Binswanger views Ellen as encircled by the greed for food and the fear of becoming fat, with all exits blocked to her. He describes her suicide as an existential act of freedom freeing her from the spell of greed and the compulsion of hunger. In resolving to commit suicide she was in a festive mood, eating lightheartedly for the first time in years, reading lyric poetry, and relishing the amusement of Mark Twain. Binswanger states that this festival of death is the result of premeditating her suicide after mature reflection, freeing herself from compulsions, dread, and fear and trembling.

COMMENTS

The modes of being–in–the–world Binswanger applies to the case of Ellen West are similar to Fairbairn's three sub-self systems. The practical-action mode comprised of Ellen's active work and creative and athletic interests would be described by Fairbairn as her central self. The aerial, ethereal free mode longing to escape the engulfment of compulsive eating is similar to Fairbairn's anti-libidinal or anti-dependent self. Her greedy compulsive self is likened to Fairbairn's libidinal, oral, greedy self. Fairbairn's sub-self systems may be considered existential modes of being-in-the-world.

Ellenberger (1958) states that Binswanger's Daseinanlyse (existential analysis) is a synthesis of psychoanalysis, phenomenology, and existential concepts. "It is a reconstruction of the inner world of experience of psychiatric patients, with the help of a conceptual framework inspired by Heidegger's studies on the structure of human existence" (p. 120). The existential philosopher William Barrett (1986) states that Heidegger's conception of the self is one of split-off, fragmented modes of being, nihilistic and essentially without hope of integration. Thus, Binswanger's theoretical framework and his case discussion leaves no hope for helping Ellen to become a whole person by integrating the split-off modes. We do not have an account of Binswanger's treatment of Ellen, but there is the suggestion that he allies himself with the aerial, ethereal, fasting self that opposed Ellen's need for nourishment. Binswanger states:

> Ellen does not want to live as the worm lives in the earth, old, ugly, dumb and dull, in a word, fat. She would rather die as a bird dies who bursts his throat with supreme jubilation or she would rather wildly consume herself in her own fire. What is new here is that the longing flashes up out of the ethereal world itself. The existential exultation itself, the festive existential joy, 'the existential fire,' are placed in the service of death, are indeed expressive of the longing for death. [p. 286]

Fairbairn's theory of split-off multiple self states differs from Binswanger's view in that object relations theory emphasizes that the split-off self states strive toward an ideal unity. Binswanger empathizes with the aerial, ethereal self's flight for freedom and autonomy but romanticizes and idealizes its destructiveness and longing for death. He is overidentified with the aerial self's struggle to repress the orally greedy self. Winnicott, in his paper "Appetite and Emotional Disorder" (1936) states:

> A discussion is overdue on the relationship of appetites to greed. I should like to put forward the suggestion that greed is never met with in the human being, even in the infant, in undisguised form, and the greediness, when it appears as a symptom, is always a secondary phenomenon, implying anxiety. Greed means to me something so primitive that it could not appear in human behavior except disguised and as part of a symptom complex. [p. 33]

Binswanger notes that Ellen says her fear of becoming fat and her fasting are the result of her greediness for food. However, he does not question whether her greed is a symptom of anxiety. He states that her greed is characterized by the closeness, narrowness, and emptiness of the world. Winnicott (1936) suggests that oral greed is precipitated by the emptiness of the self. Balint (1968) describes the basic fault as an inner emptiness giving rise to addictive states and oral greed.

Today, Ellen West would be diagnosed as anorexic. These patients display the characteristics I have described as typical of the schizoid condition. Wilson (1986) states that anorexics do not suffer from the generalized ego weakness of the borderline patient. Rather, there is a split in the ego, a part of which is pseudo-normal with adaptive ability for observation of the self and the environment and passively compliant toward overbearing parents, especially in academic functioning, the performance of familial tasks, and so on. This pseudo-normal, compliant self is identical to Winnicott's concept of the false self and Fairbairn's view of the role-playing central self. Wilson suggests that the pseudo-normal self reinforces the splitting off of the sadomasochistic oral dependency conflicts manifested in the anorexic symptoms. Food becomes symbolic of love for the anorexic. Winnicott (1963) remarks on the relationship between severe anorexic symptoms and an underlying schizoid condition. He points out that these patients often manifest anorexic symptoms in infancy. Ellen West rejected milk and then food, beginning at nine months.

In discussing the case of Ellen West, Schoenewolf points out that both parents seem to have been strongly and overly controlling and that this behavior may have caused her to reject milk at nine months. Although Binswanger provides scanty information about the parents' attitudes in Ellen's history, their overly controlling behavior can be reconstructed in their interference with her later engagement. Shortly after this incident, Ellen became depressed, felt that she was fat, and began to fast. Eigen (1986) suggests that Ellen was lacking control and autonomy and could only express her rage and assert control in the area of food intake.

The anorexic's refusal of food also points to her anxiety concerning invasiveness (Sours 1980). Winnicott's notion of the secret self's need to remain inviolate, incommunicado, and isolated is relevant. The parent's overly controlling behavior threatened to violate the secret self. Ellen states she is not going to be a puppet or submissive. She identifies with the underprivileged masses who are exploited and violated. She remarks that her first analyst spoke the truth in his remarks concerning her tyranny over other persons. However, her domineering behavior served to defend her against being dominated. She rejects her analyst's interpretations of her anal and oedipal conflicts. Winnicott remarks that in his work with an anorexic patient, he learned how the patient had to reject interpretations made out of the analyst's cleverness in order to protect the secret self. Ellen's strong oppositionalism, manifested in her refusal to accept that a bird's nest was a bird's nest, revealed her acute anxiety about the violation of the secret self and being made into a passive object. She rejected the internalization of the object by an identification with the rigid, controlling, tyrannical parental figures. She was caught in a vicious cycle, whereby her rejection of a potentially invasive object to protect the secret self resulted in the inner emptiness of the basic fault, which gave rise to oral greed, which in turn had to be rejected through the anorexic restriction. It will be recalled that in her work as a social worker she was especially interested in nourishing her clients. Thus, she projected the hungry self state into the needy clients and fed it vicariously through nurturing them.

ELLEN'S IDEA OF THINNESS AND THE TRANSFORMATIONAL OBJECT

Ellen West's ideal of extreme thinness can be explicated in terms of Bollas' theory of the transformational object. Bollas (1987) says that the infant's subjective object (Winnicott 1963) is originally a transformational object. The caregiver originally relates to the infant through processes that transform the baby's internal and external environment. This comprehensive mother is termed the environment mother because she is the total environment for the infant. The mother is originally less identifiable as an object than as a process related to internal and external transformations. Bollas states "A transformational object is experientially identified by the infant with processes that alter self experience" (p. 14). The object is originally known not as an "object representation" but rather as a recurrent experience of being—an existential as opposed to representational mode of knowing. The concept of mother being experienced as transformation is supported by the fact that she performs the function of altering the environment to meet his needs. This aspect of early life lives on in certain modes of object-seeking in adult life in which the object is pursued as a medium that alters the self. In ordinary development the transformational process is displaced from the mothering environment to various subjective objects and to the transitional phase. Residues of the transformational period may remain in adult life in the hope invested in various objects such as a new home, a new job, a move, a vacation, or a new relationship, all of which may signify the quest for a transitional experience. The expectation of being transformed by such an object may inspire the individual with an idealizing, sacred attitude toward it. Therefore, in adult life, the quest for the transformational object is to remember an early self-and-object experience, not cognitively but existentially, through a positive affective experience that is identified with transformational experiences of the past.

In normative development, only a trace or residue remains of the transformational object in adult life. Schizoid pathology emerges from a failure to be disillusioned in the magical hope that a transformational object will be the salvation of the self. Bollas states that the gambler's game, the perfect crime, the search for the perfect woman or the ideal man may reflect continuing pathological ties to the transformational object. The schizoid search for the transformational object is associated with ego transformation and the repair of the "basic fault." There is the conviction that the actual mother will never provide the supplies, and she is therefore replaced by an act that represents the relationship to the primary caregiver, but which endeavors to transform the patient's ego into an omnipotent, self-sufficient state. In Dostoyevski's *Crime and Punishment*, Raskolnikov manifests the search for the transformational object in his belief that if he commits the perfect murder he becomes a superman. The schizoid patient may manifest the search for a pathological transformational object through any object, including the quest for a job, a home, a school, a baby, a perfect report card, the perfect mate, wealth, the ideal aesthetic experience, writing the perfect novel, and so forth. What distinguishes the pathological transformational object in ordinary adult life is that the schizoid patient believes he achieves a state of omnipotence by fulfilling the pursuit, and if he fails, he feels empty, apathetically depressed, and that life holds no meaning or purpose.

Ellen West pursued the transformational object in her act of becoming extremely thin. Her fasting, the need to achieve perfect grades in school, the strenuous exercises and hikes she undertook, were reflective of her efforts to become omnipotent and self-sufficient without needs. The ideal of thinness is described by Binswanger in terms of Ellen becoming weightless, defying gravity, flying above humanity in her ethereal state. Thus, similarly to Raskolnikov, Ellen's quest for the transformational object was a wish for superiority, to become a superwoman, expressed in the metaphor of rising above the animalistic, biological needs of humanity. The wish to become aerial was a wish to become pure "soul," divorced from the body. In schizoid patients, a pathological narcissistic personality sometimes serves in an effort to repair the basic fault. The patient John, discussed earlier was also in pursuit of a transformational object in the obsession with his secretary, Liz. John experienced her as a transformational object in his belief that she gave him a reason for living and for going into the world each day.

Winnicott (1962) states that the schizoid patient may experience a therapeutic regression to repair the basic fault. In this experience, the therapeutic setting itself becomes the transformational holding environment that alters the patient's ego state. Ellen West expressed a need for therapeutic regression in her second analysis before entering Binswanger's clinic. She wished to lay her head on the analyst's shoulder and for him to say "Ellen, my child." The analyst understood her wish only in terms of the oedipal conflict and the erotic transference toward the paternal imago and did not see her wish for dependence on the transformational holding object.

OBJECT RELATIONS: EROS AND THANATOS

Binswanger says that the wish to die runs throughout Ellen West's entire life. Loewald (1973) states that most American psychoanalysts have objected to Freud's concept of the death instinct because of its biological and pessimistic outlook. In England, Klein accepted the death instinct, but the British object relations theorists, Fairbairn, Guntrip, and Winnicott, objected to the Kleinian view, which stated that the strength of the biological death drive greatly influenced and shaped the individual's relations with the object world. Loewald contends that it is not as easy or as warranted as many analysts believe to reject Freud's theory of the life and death instincts. He believes that the death instinct is clinically manifest and pervasively evident in the propensity for inner conflict, the need for suffering, violent destructiveness toward the self and the object, the intractable unconscious sense of guilt and some somatic illnesses, physical decline, and withdrawal states. Loewald states that whether or not Freud was influenced by Nietzsche, Freud understood inner conflict in terms of a thesis put forth by Nietzsche in *Genealogy of Morals,* namely, as the result of a process of turning inward of man's aggressiveness in the course of man's development from a primitive state to a civilized one. Freud (1937) stated that the internal conflicts were the equivalents to the external struggles that ceased. Loewald points out that this internalization was originally a defense against the dangers of external aggression, but later, in accord with Hartmann's (1950) concept of change of function, the internalized struggle became the hallmark of psychic structure. In fact, Fairbairn's view of the origin of psychic structure based on the internalization of frustrating object relations recapitulates in individual psychic development the phylogenetic evolution of internalization described by Loewald.

Loewald presents an object relations theory of the life and death instincts that he believes removes many of the objections to the postulation of the death instinct. Loewald (1972) states that in his approach, the life and death instincts cannot be seen as biological variables, independent of the early environmental constellations. Granting the duality of life and death instincts, they are resultants of primitive interactions with the external object world and derive their form, their flexibility, or rigidity, as well as their capacity for higher transformation, from the early formative object relations interactions. The intensity of intractable destructive tendencies would depend primarily on early environmental actions that favored a distorted organization of the destructive and libidinal drives and the lack of balance between them. Loewald's formulations are similar to Jacobson's (1964) belief that the undifferentiated drives are organized and formed under the influence of pleasurable and unpleasurable external object relations. However, Jacobson rejected the theory of a life and death drive, believing that there could be neither primary narcissism or primary masochism, given that the self-representation developed only after a prolonged period of undifferentiation. The views of the British theorists (Fairbairn 1944, Klein 1946) and the new infant research (Stern 1985) suggest that there is pristine but unitary sense of self and object from earliest infancy. Therefore, it would be possible for libidinal and destructive forces to be organized and formed around self-and-object interactions from birth.

Ellen West's drive toward death occurred in the context of object relations in accordance with Loewald's views. For instance, Binswanger states that she fantasized about death as personified in the form of a beautiful woman, white asters in her hair, with deep grey eyes. Ellen experienced the longing for death as an urge to merge with this object and that through death, she would achieve the greatest happiness. She emphasizes that in her mind, death is not pictured as a man but as a woman. The alluring appeal of the female personification of death has the quality of the exciting, tempting, internal object. Fairbairn (1940) described the schizoid patient's exciting internal object as based upon the exciting nongratifying aspects of the early caregiver. Ellen's attraction to this alluring object has the quality of the symbiotic need for the primary caregiver. Ellen's striving to become thin, aerial, ethereal, to become pure spirit divorced from the body, is ultimately a striving for death. It will be recalled that Ellen identified with the view that the Gods love those who die young. Thus she becomes lovable through death and merges with the symbiotic object. Earlier it was mentioned that the ideal of becoming thin is the transformational object that alters Ellen's ego state. Now it can be seen that the ultimate transformational object for Ellen is death itself, which thinness is a way station toward, death transforming her into a lovable object and thereby magically repairing the basic fault. Fairbairn's theory that libido serves the connection with objects is in accord with Freud's later dual-drive instinctual theory (1949) in which the life instinct is manifested by eros, which binds together separate entities into ever-greater unities. Freud's theory of the death instinct is that thanatos serves to undo connections. In this author's view, the death instinct serves the secret self's need to remain isolated, incommunicado, protected from impingement. Sutherland (1990) remarked on Fairbairn's neglect of the infant's ordinary rejective, aggressive behavioral tendencies. The life instinct serves the opposing need for communication. If the secret self is actually invaded and violated, the death drive—the need to sever connections—becomes dominant. Thus, Ellen's opposition to her biological needs and her social community reflects the expression of the death drive manifested as aggression to protect the secret self from further invasiveness.

Fairbairn (1940) remarks that in the case of the schizoid patient, the caregiver is unable to respond to his need for primary love and communicates that his need for love is destructive. The infant's need intensifies with the lack of gratification and becomes transformed into the destructive death drive by virtue of the object's viewing the need as destructive. Therefore, in the case of the schizoid patient, the death drive is not only organized around protecting the secret self from protection but also around the need for connection and love. Thus, the libidinal need for the object is felt to be serving a destructive end. Ellen believes that libidinal gratification results in the emptying and destruction of the object and the emptying and destruction of the self. The libidinal need for connection was submerged by the death drive and death itself became the alluring, symbiotic object.

In Loewald's theory, the life and death drives are not

biological instincts but rather strictly psychological forces. In rejecting the death instinct, classical psychoanalysis has neglected to fully study the anxiety over objectlessness, nothingness, nihilation, and destruction that are expressed by this force. Instead, classical analysis primarily focused upon the experiences expressed by the life instinct in the study of the ego and its efforts at adaptation. This ego psychological focus was important and valuable but sometimes weakened by not sufficiently drawing attention to its dialectical relationship to nothingness, destructiveness, and so forth.

The empty core is the experience of lack in biological need that becomes structured into the psyche as desire. As Sartre (1948) points out, all imaginary objects or images are an absence. The human infant has both incorporative and rejective tendencies at birth. The incorporative tendencies result in the sense of fulfillment and the rejective tendencies result in the sense of emptiness. Fulfillment and emptiness are in constant dialectical relationship to one another, each feeding and stimulating the other. The life drive is the force for fulfillment, and the death drive is the force behind emptiness, expulsion, and separation from the object.

Fairbairn described object relations as crucial in rescuing the beleaguered self. He is referring to cooperative sharing as a biological source to our social tendencies. A film by Akira Kurosawa, *Ikiru,* speaks to this issue. The film depicts a middle-aged civil service bureaucrat who is depicted as schizoid, in the sense that his life is one of passing time without purpose or direction, with little enthusiasm or vitality for any activities or the demands of living. In fact, the bureaucrat is nicknamed by workers in his department as "the mummy." One day, the mummy discovers that he has terminal cancer with only a few months to live. Initially he gets drunk and seeks the nightlife of the city to escape his woes. The mummy is awakened to the fact that he wants to live and that he has lived a living death throughout his life. There are a group of impoverished citizens that have been pleading with the government office for a public park but they are continually sent from one government office to the next without any satisfaction. The mummy finds a purpose in living by helping the poor public citizens win the public park. His concern for their plight awakens him to live and provides him with an energy and persistence he never knew in life. After his death, the deputy mayor, in his pathological narcissism, assumes the credit for the public park to further his career. The other bureaucrats cannot believe that the former colleague had assisted the poor citizens without any reward. Thus Kurosawa depicts the dying bureaucrat as overcoming the absurdity of existence and nihilism through mature object relations. This view cannot be taken lightly. In the Holocaust, the persons who had the greatest chance of survival were those individuals who did not lose their humanity even under the most nihilistic conditions, and who, in the face of starvation or death, preserved their capacity for concern by sharing with others a tiny morsel of bread or the warmth of their clothing.

Taking precedes giving in developmental chronology. The individual must be given and must take in enough love, he must know how to take care of himself, how to say no when necessary, to be secure and to enjoy his own intake. Then there is a natural inclination to give or to give back. Giving may be through a gift to posterity, the invention of something useful, a discovery; through teaching, parenting, love relations, or friendship. It is this generativity, this giving and taking with love that enables us to overcome the absurdity and nihilism that is also a pervasive, inherent part of human existence. Such would be a view that I refer to as "existential object relations."

7

CONFRONTATION OF THE SCHIZOID PATIENT

This chapter will present techniques that address the schizoid patient's object relations that reflect self-destruction. The therapist has the difficult therapeutic task of confronting the patient's self-destruction in a way that demonstrates the therapist's caring and protective attitude. I believe that there is a current trend in the field that either supports or disclaims empathic and confrontative techniques, viewing them as mutually exclusive.

THE EMPATHIC RESPONSE TO THE SCHIZOID PATIENT

Kohut (1984) defines empathy as the ability to experience the inner life of another person. The analyst's empathic response to the patient is comparable to the parental object's empathic response to the infant. Kohut (1984) states, "The baby is anxious and the mother experiences a taste of the baby's anxiety; she picks up the baby and holds it close. As a result of this sequence, the mother has experienced as an empathic signal not the baby's total anxiety, but only a diminished view of it" (pp. 82–83).

Bion (1962) provides a similar view of the infant–mother relationship as the prototype of the analyst's empathic response in his conception of the "container." Bion states that the infant projects an unwanted part of the psyche, its bad feelings or bad self, into the good breast. The mother (or good breast from the infant's subjective viewpoint) contains and modifies the infant's projected bad feelings so that the infant eventually reintrojects the unwanted, bad feelings. Bion states that the maternal containing function allows for the infant's bad feelings to become tolerable to the infant's psyche. Thus Kohut's "empathy" and Bion's containing function are comparable ideas that relate to the mother's capacity to experience a diminished version of the infant's panic while remaining relatively calm and thereby calming the infant. If the caregiver has a tendency to respond with panic to the infant's anxiety, she may inappropriately distance herself from the infant or become distressed herself. In either case, she deprives the infant of the opportunity of the merger experience in which she returns from her signal anxiety to a calm state, thereby calming him.

Kohut (1971) states, "The analyst adapts his empathic response to the level of narcissistic regression and the developmental needs of the patient" (p. 92). The empathic response is comprised of mirroring the patient's early narcissistic grandiosity or accepting the patient's developmental need to merge with an omnipotent object.

Kohut (1977) states that the child's need for an empathic environment to be attuned to his emotional needs is analogous to the newborn infant's physiological need for oxygen. Balint (1968) states that the infant's need for primary love is comparable to the need for oxygen. Thus empathy and primary love are identical concepts referring to the nascent self's need to take in the holding environment.

Kohut (1971) describes the schizoid patient as being in danger of uncontrollable regression if his need for human closeness emerges. Kohut states that the schizoid patient experienced failure in the formation of the nuclear self in earliest development as a result of failures in parenting that collaborated with constitutional factors in the patient. Regression as the result of narcissistic injury may go beyond archaic narcissism and result in the fragmentation of the self. Kohut's discussion of the failure in the formation of the nuclear self and the danger of fragmentation in regression is reminiscent of Balint's view of the basic fault and the collapse of the ego. Kohut (1971), similarly to the British theorists, states that the schizoid patient's retreat from human closeness is not caused by a primary inability to love or disinterest in relationships, but rather because of an accurate evaluation of his emotional fragility and the danger of regression.

Kohut (1971) rightfully recommends a psychoanalytically oriented psychotherapy procedure that respects the patient's need to maintain distance in the transference and to concentrate libidinal investments in activities that minimize human involvement (for instance, creative work or the study of theoretical or metaphysical subjects). Kohut recognizes that the schizoid patient is in need of an empathic therapeutic response but also cautions that empathy could promote overwhelming object hunger that may set in motion transference regression resulting in severe fragmentation. In fact, Kohut states that the patient is constantly in danger of uncontrollable regression, which he staves off by retreating from human closeness in all areas of life.

It is my view that the therapist may provide empathy toward the schizoid patient and allow for therapeutic regression if he also confronts and interprets the patient's destructive tendencies. The confrontation of destructive patterns may prevent an uncontrollable, destructive regression. Confrontations are most effective when the therapist develops a strong, empathic bond with the patient.

Searles critiques Kohut for not confronting the patient's aggressive tendencies. Searles (1986) states, "I wish merely to emphasize, however, that whereas Kohut does quite full justice to the patient's need for responses in the realm of empathic tact, gentleness and, in essence, kindly acceptance on the part of the analyst, he dwells in his books (Kohut 1971, 1977) scarcely at all upon the patient's equally great need for well-timed responses of a very aggressive sort, indeed, from the analyst" (p. 382).

Searles's view on the patient's need for the analyst's aggressive responses is identical to Winnicott's ideas on "hate in the countertransference." Winnicott (1947) states that the severely disturbed patient's destructive behavior may create situations in which the analyst is justified in feeling objective hatred toward the patient. Often, the analyst must tolerate hating the patient but doing nothing about it. However, there are occasions when the therapist remains conscious of his own objective hatred and uses this aggression to respond forcefully to curtail the patient's destructiveness. I do not think that Winnicott means to justify a therapist's sadism, giving the patient a dose of his own medicine, or narcissistically injuring the patient. Hate may be an expression of empathy when aggression is utilized to serve a protective function.

Winnicott (1947) states that there are times when the patient seeks the therapist's hate and needs a response of objective hatred. Sometimes, the patient can only believe that he is loved or cared for after he has sought and reached the analyst's hatred. When the therapist confronts the patient's destructiveness, he expresses his concern and regard for the patient. Sometimes it is only after such confrontations that the patient can believe in the therapist's kind, gentle, mirroring responses. The following clinical vignette illustrates the techniques of confronting the patient's destructiveness.

THE CASE OF ANNETTE

Presenting Crisis

Annette was a young adult of Italian origin who lived with her parents while attending college on a full-time basis. She had been bulimic, binging and purging, for seven years. Recently, her eating disorder had been getting worse. She had at least three bulimic episodes daily. She began to date a young man and had hopes of being saved from a lifelong depression through this new relationship. The young man left her after a few weeks and Annette became seriously depressed. She went to a mental health clinic. Unfortunately, her therapist had to leave the clinic because of a personal crisis. He had assured Annette that she would be reassigned a new therapist, but she persisted in her concerns. She returned home and asked her mother if a person who committed suicide could go to heaven. The mother, a Catholic, replied in the affirmative. Later that evening, she was found in a coma from an overdose of sleeping medication.

She was psychiatrically hospitalized for several weeks. She said that throughout her life, she had suicide ideation but never believed she would act upon it. Since the suicide attempt, something had been set off in her mind. It was as if an inner demon actively and constantly tempted her to die. She told the staff she wanted to be discharged but also that she wanted to die. She talked about her release. She had told the psychiatrist that she never broke promises. He convinced her to agree not to kill herself for thirty days and hoped that after that interval, the intensity of the wish to die would diminish.

Annette was discharged and returned to the clinic where she had originally been seen, and she commenced treatment with me.

Concerned about her intense death wish, I referred her to a research and treatment program for bulimia and underlying major depression that provided psychopharmacological treatment. Annette was disqualified because of her suicidal history. However, the consulting psychiatrist concurred about the severity of the case and referred her privately.

Annette met with the psychiatrist and was open about the severity of her symptoms and the intensity of her wish to die. The psychiatrist did not want to start her on medication immediately. He felt that she had complete faith that the medication would immediately relieve her of all pain and that she would be disappointed and possibly become even more depressed. He also felt that her suicidal tendencies were so acute that she could not be trusted to take the medication appropriately or might mix it with alcohol. The medication might tip the balance in the direction of suicide. He attempted to talk her into being rehospitalized. She adamantly refused. She also began to deny what she had previously told him as to the severity of her condition. The case presented a dilemma. The psychiatrist thought medication could help, but as long as she remained outside of a hospital he wanted her to be stabilized before beginning the medication. She was informed that she would be seen by the therapist three times weekly in intensive psychotherapy for this purpose and every three weeks by a psychiatrist to evaluate her readiness for medication. The psychotherapy served as preparation. This therapist had the unusual task of helping her become less self-destructive so that she could make appropriate use of psychopharmacological treatment. There were therapeutic object relations interventions utilized for this purpose.

Personal History

The patient grew up in an intact family with a sister five years older than she. Her mother had a history of chronic, clinical depression and had recently been placed on medication. The mother went to work full-time during Annette's first year of life. Annette was left in the care of neighbors, friends, and relatives. The mother did not want to work because of her depression. She also did not want to leave her child. It was at her husband's insistence that she went to work. He said that the only way that they could overcome their financial troubles was if she worked full-time. The parents were known to the same agency where Annette was receiving treatment, so there was a detailed family history.

The mother seemed to be a well-meaning but ineffectual person who was overwhelmed by her depression and the demands of living. Her husband had grown up in an orphanage and was a needy, infantile man. After marrying and starting a family, he still spent weekends with his former motorcycle gang. He was a narcissistic, critical man who expected the females in the family to serve him and constantly berated them for not living up to his demands. Although he did not physically abuse his wife, he constantly verbally abused family members. The mother dealt with him by becoming withholding and detached from him. Because of his neediness, he could not tolerate her withdrawal and became contrite and remorseful. Annette said that it appeared that he held all the reins of power. Annette's mother was not without power and could quietly turn his neediness against him.

Father was obsessed with breasts and with having his dependency needs met. Annette astutely recognized that his neediness related to his oral deprivation in his childhood. She had taken psychology courses and learned that as an orphan he longed for the good breast. The father had fondled her breasts and her older sister's as they became pubescent. The girls had told the mother, who spoke with him so that he discontinued this behavior, but Annette had remained uncomfortable in the father's presence. It was at this time that she developed the bulimic symptom.

Annette had endeavored to be an outstanding student. She worked diligently for excellent marks and would be inappropriately upset if she did not achieve them. As long as she worked hard and performed successfully, she was pleased and cheerful. She was hypersensitive to others' opinions and overly self-critical. She had appeared passive and compliant, but could be willful and obstinate by withdrawing from the object world. She had ended long-standing, seemingly close relationships with girlfriends after minor rifts and would not mend the friendships. Her cheerful affect would quickly change to depression when faced with small disappointments. Since late adolescence, she had taken dance classes and was constantly critical of her weight and agility. Thus, Annette attacked herself for not living up to inordinate self-expectations. She suffered from an eating disorder, severe depression, and withdrawn behavior.

Direct Intervention with the Inner Demon

At the beginning of treatment following discharge from the hospital, Annette would come to sessions upset. She said that she deserved to die because she had fallen behind in school, burdened her parents, and overate. In the following weeks, as she returned to her daily activities, she would cry that she deserved to die because she was fatter and less graceful than the other dancers in her class, had received a grade of B, not an A, because she overate, and because her father was critical of her slovenly dress, messy room, and poor table manners. I intervened by asking, "What would you think of someone who went around murdering people who did not receive A's in school, who did not dance perfectly, or who neglected dress, table manners, or the bedroom?" I added, "I mean this concretely. Think of a serial murderer who went around murdering for these reasons. What would you think?"

She laughed and acknowledged, "That person would be crazy."

I then pointed out that she had such a "killer" existing in her mind, persecuting and threatening her, saying that she deserved to die for minor infractions. When we viewed the situation "objectively," this way of thinking was crazy.

She said that she pictured this informal persecuting voice as a crazy-looking woman, holding a club and threatening her. She added that it sounded like an abusive parent.

Given the seriousness of the situation, I called in the parents and obtained their agreement to come in on an as-needed basis. I told them how vulnerable their daughter was and that she was capable of killing herself. I also told the father that his critical remarks reinforced her self-hatred and could push her over the edge. My remarks strengthened the position of the mother, who was more concerned about Annette. She now felt justified in telling the father to stop his criticisms of Annette or at least to state them constructively. The parents left with an agreement to temporarily stop all criticism. They felt that I understood that they were burdened with the care of an emotionally ill adult daughter, but also that I conveyed that if the father continued to attack her, he must want her dead.

Empathy and Confrontation

In the midst of berating herself for her failings, Annette stated that the only occasions that she had felt better were occasional quiet times with her mother, who allowed her to complain. She was reluctant to go to her mother because she knew how burdened and depressed she was. But since I had met with the parents, the mother made more of an effort to sit with her and inquire about her life. This unburdening was good medicine, but Annette feared draining her mother, overwhelming her, or wearing her out. I interpreted that Annette needed to use her mother to hold her negative feelings but was unsure if her mother was strong enough to manage without falling apart.

Annette became aware of her disappointed need for her mother. She reproached herself for her room being a mess, for the neglect of her appearance, her weight, and her room. I interpreted, "You are feeling the presence of the absence of your mother. The neglect of yourself is a communication that you still need your mother to take care of you. It is a plea for her not to abandon you. You also feel that no matter what you do, fix yourself up, clean your room, it will not bring her to you."

On occasion, we would argue about whether she deserved to die.

Annette: I am struggling all of the time. Yesterday I thought of doing it. I know someone I could buy pills from. I looked in the medicine chest. There are no more pills. They got rid of them after they spoke to you.

Therapist: You wanted to see if they wanted you to live or to die—if they at least cared enough to get rid of the pills. What made you feel suicidal yesterday?

Annette: I always wanted to die. But yesterday, I received a C in biology. I hardly studied. My parents send me to school and I am not doing anything. I am a burden to everyone. I'll fall further behind in school.

Therapist: The idea that you deserve to die for receiving a C is that crazy, sadistic, tyrant inside of you. Only a sadistic killer would think someone deserved to die for a C. If someone tried to kill another person for receiving a C, even if a parent tried to kill a child, they would lock him up. You do not deserve to die for a C. That side of yourself is being beaten into giving up and becoming hopeless. It is vulnerable and weak and needs protection, not abuse. It only gets a C because it is communicating it needs help, it is mourning for a parent's love, and it has given up on winning a parent's love by doing well. It has no hope of becoming the object of a parent's desire and love. That side of you needs to be nurtured and not attacked. We need to do that through this relationship.

The patient's cruel self-reproaches reflect an identification with the bad object, which is a composite of both unloving parents. Next, the therapist interprets that the patient who is weak and vulnerable tries to feel powerful by assuming the identity of the tyrant parent and not the tyrannized. The therapist then remarks that the patient also secretly hated the parental image she identified with. Thus, the wish to kill oneself is also a wish to kill the inner demon, to quiet its persecutions for once and for all. It is as if the persecutory inner demons continually taunt: "You deserve to die for being such a miserable wretch," and the persecuted self finally says "All right, if that is the case, I will finally end the misery of this miserable wretch, but the joke is really on you, since I kill you if I kill me." This is the intervention I made with Annette. Sometimes, she preferred not to talk in sessions, remarking "There is no use to talking, things are miserable, I am wretched and nothing can help." At other times she would ceaselessly go over all of her failures or her despicable life, denigrating herself, her circumstances, and me. Then, I could not get through with interpretations. I felt hate in the countertransference based upon my helplessness and her communication that she felt wretched and might kill herself, but there was nothing she would do to help herself or allow me to do.

I said, "Unfortunately you are absolutely correct. If you refuse to look at what is making you feel this way, if you will not even talk, or reflect on what is going on with yourself, if you remain totally at one with hating yourself and defeating yourself, then this cannot help. It is not helping because you are not cooperating. You are completely closing off from me and the vulnerable part of yourself that needs help. You are telling it and me that nothing can help, so we should give up. In prophesizing that nothing can change, you maintain everything as unchanged. You shut out all communication but then feel deprived and as if nothing is helping.

Annette: But it has not helped. I've been coming here a month.

Therapist: A month is not enough time, and it will not help unless you try to make it help by looking at what is happening and why you're withdrawing this way. The purpose of this is to look at yourself, to understand what is going on. So when you feel completely destructive or hopeless, the thing is not to go entirely with that feeling, but to look at what makes you feel that way, thereby beginning to separate yourself from it.

Annette: I don't know if I can.

Therapist: Of course you don't. You have no experience doing it. It is brand-new. You are just going with the destructive feeling, speaking to yourself in the voice of negatives and hopelessness. You are withdrawing and saying that you do not want to take in what goes on here just as you do not take in food.

In this way I endeavor to illustrate that her oral conflicts about taking in or rejecting the breast (food) is becoming activated in the transference resistance.

The Dangers of Supporting the Patient in Perfectionist Functioning

The case of Annette, like the case of Ellen West, illustrates the dangers in joining and in supporting the patient's perfect-ionistic efforts. An orientation that stresses behavioral goals could result in the therapist supporting patients like Annette's need for As, to improve her dancing, to straighten her room, and the like. The therapist might even say something such as, "What can you do to improve your grades?" and help the patient to develop a behavioral plan in this direction. With these patients, achieving high grades, exercising, and compulsive acts are symptoms. Annette's aspirations were obviously perfectionistic and destructive. However, there are schizoid patients who do not enter treatment as disturbed and suicidal, and therefore their perfectionistic symptoms may be mistaken for reasonable efforts at adaptive functioning. The standard treatment of borderline patients often involves overt support of adaptive individuated strivings and confrontation of dependency needs. This approach could be disastrous with a schizoid patient like Annette. She needs guidance and mirroring of adaptive individuation but only in the context of differentiating and disarming pathologically perfectionistic symptoms.

When a patient is seriously suicidal or motivated by intense pathological perfectionism, it is imperative for the therapist to confront the sadism, tyranny, and craziness of the internal sadistic object directly and constantly. Once I identify the homicidal nature of the client's identification with the parental object, I do not hesitate to state that this part of the patient is crazy, sadistic, and tyrannical. These confrontations could literally save the patient's life. The confrontations are accompanied by my actively assuming a protective stance toward the vulnerable infantile self and showing that its "death sentence" is not warranted. Only as the infantile self allies itself to me do I empathically address the patient's need to identify with an abusive object and persecute the infantile self in order to achieve a sense of power in the only way this object knows know.

Annette's Plan to Sacrifice Herself for the Parents

Annette brought into the treatment her belief that her actual parents wished for her death. It was inevitable that this would occur since the bad object's homicidal ideation was based upon this perception.

Annette came into session after a few months of treatment and announced, "Today is my last session."

Therapist: Why?

Annette: I've decided that I'll leave therapy and decide when the time is right for me to kill myself.

It flashed through my mind that Annette had left a session with her previous therapist and tried to kill herself.

Annette: I have no purpose. I'm just a burden. My parents have nothing because of me. I have squandered their money on college and I am accomplishing nothing. They work to house and feed me. All of my life, all I have done is take, take. At least, if I kill myself, they can take a vacation. They will be able to go away in a couple of months. I don't want to hold them back. Their lives will be much better without me. I won't be in their way. They will not have to worry about me.

Therapist: You are insinuating that you feel your parents do not love you.

Annette: (makes a puzzled face) What do you mean? They love me too much. They're ruining their lives for me.

Therapist: You are describing your parents as witches out of a fairy tale who do not love their child.

Annette: (puzzled) What?

Therapist: What kind of parents would go off on a vacation months after their daughter's suicide and have the time of their lives? You are saying they could only have a happy life predicated upon the death of their child by her own hand. What kind of parents would want their child to die so that they could have more money? It sounds to me as if you are telling me your parents resemble the cruel parents that you find in a fairy tale. I'm thinking of something like Hansel and Gretel. They abandon their children to be baked in a witch's oven because they no longer want the responsibility. So you are saying that they want you dead and you will accommodate them to send them on vacation and give them one less mouth to feed and house.

Annette was quite shaken up by what I said. At first she argued. I didn't say the full statement at one time. She questioned in disbelief. I said more and I said it again until it amounted to the entire statement. She sat with her mouth wide open and said this is shock therapy. There was a pause. She said, "I can see the point of what you are saying. I didn't think of it that way. I'm confused." I said that I had no intention of allowing her to leave to kill herself to accommodate what she believed her parents wanted. I told her that if she was correct and they wanted her dead to go off on vacation, they were evil parents or crazy parents, much like the parents in fairy tales. I said it was my job to protect her from them and from herself and have her placed in a hospital. She assured me in every way that she no longer intended to kill herself. She said that she did not believe her parents wanted her to die so that they could go on a vacation. She believed that they cared about her even though they had problems. However, she could see that what she had said to me implied that they did not care about her and

wanted her to die. She wondered if on some level she believed
they did not care. There was something concerning her. When
she tried to kill herself the last time, she had asked her mother
beforehand whether a suicide victim could go to heaven. The
mother, a religious Catholic, replied "yes." What did that
mean? Did her mother want her dead? She cried for a prolonged period, saying no one cared about her. I asked if she felt
I didn't care and she replied that I proved I did by struggling
with her about this today. She said she meant her parents did
not love her. She left.

Later that day I received a call from her mother. She said
she was alarmed that Annette never returned home after the
session. She recalled what I had said about Annette being in
danger. "Did Annette leave all right?" she asked. Annette
arrived home shortly after. Her mother was hysterical. Annette called and said she just arrived home; she stopped off at
the library, and her mother was upset with worry. Annette
sounded absolutely gleeful that her mother cared.

The Patient Fitting the Role
of a Dead Object to the Caregiver

In the ensuing sessions, Annette talked about her early familial
relationships to better understand her current relationships.
She remembered her mother as being clinically depressed. Her
mother was always a binge eater, but not a purger. Her mother
was forced to work full-time and felt it was too much, given
her emotional fragility. The mother was also overburdened in
trying to meet the excessive neediness of her infantile husband.
Annette's mother would come home exhausted and collapse
upon the bed. Annette felt that she could not ask for anything
emotional from her. The mother's message was, "Be quiet, be
perfect because I am dead tired." Annette tried to cooperate. In
turn, the mother could love her for leaving her alone. The
mother would always say, "She is a wonderful child, she
leaves me alone." Thus, Annette learned that she would not be
abandoned if she was inert. The mother mirrored her for being

compliant. If she needed anything, the mother gave her food. The giving of things was not out of love, but just to placate her. At other times, when the mother felt depressed, Annette would lift the mother's spirits by becoming lively and gay. Annette's liveliness was never for herself, only for the object. The problem became that to be a quiet person was equivalent to being dead. As an infant, she felt her mother was "dead tired." Thus, she identified with her mother in her deadness. As long as she received good grades, had friends, and did not make demands, the relationship with the mother worked.

Winnicott (1963) states that usually in the infant's development, the mother has live internal objects and the infant fits into the mother's image of a live child. In certain cases in which the mother is depressed, her internal object is dead at the crucial period of the child's infancy. Winnicott (1963) states: "here the infant has to fit in with the role of a *dead* object, or else has to be lively to counteract the mother's preconception with the idea of the child's deadness" (pp. 191–192).

I interpreted directly. "You have been made to feel that your mother, worn out with living, wanted you to be a quiet baby. This meant being a dead baby in order to be loved and not abandoned. At other times your mother felt 'dead' in her depression and you had to be lively. You did not feel loved as a person in your own right."

I once told her that I did not want her to be a dead baby. I wanted her to be alive. She said that I was not her parent and she was not my daughter. I agreed, adding that in therapy there is a symbolic child–parent relationship in our mutual effort to help her overcome the obstacles to her growth. Annette marked this session as an important factor in helping her to overcome her life-and-death conflict. She said to think of herself as my symbolic daughter made her feel alive. For the first time, she realized that she could relive being a child, only now a live child who grows into an adult. Then she added, "This is not reliving, I have never been a child." She did not realize that being a child was a foundation for becoming an adult.

Annette finished college and left her family to live on her own. I treated her for nearly four years and the last I heard she was well. After she got in touch with the issue of the dead baby, she was no longer suicidal. She then started on medication, which further lessened her depression.

Implications

Annette did not turn to the primary object only for need gratification but also to contain disturbing affective states (Bion 1967). Therefore, when we speak of the infant's need to be loved as a person in its own right (Fairbairn 1940), need includes not only gratifications, comforting, and mirroring, but also the containing function.

The above case illustrates that when the parental object could not respond with the containing function, the infant died somewhat, psychically, by becoming an affectless baby. Balint (1968) describes an inner deadness as characteristic of the "basic fault." The well-known inner deadness of the schizoid patient is the result of efforts to become a dead baby in order to be loved and not abandoned by the object. This action of becoming dead becomes structured into the psyche as the basic fault. When the object rejects the infant's needs, the child finds the object unresponsive or dead. Thus the "dead baby" identity is also an identification with a dead mother. The schizoid patient's efforts to become a thing-in-itself and not fully human, or its relating to another person as an "it" and not fully human, are aspects of this inner deadness. The infant experiences the parent's rejection of its need as a wish on the parent's part, that the infant would be without needs.

Annette reveals information about the schizoid patient's family relationships. The mother is neglectful, not abusive. It is primarily neglect in the first year of life that is responsible for schizoid states. An individual who has borderline and schizoid features usually suffers both abuse and neglect. The abuse relates to the borderline states, and the neglect accounts for the schizoid states. Annette's mother is ambivalent. Although she tells her that suicides go to heaven, she later looked for her when she did not appear. At home Annette receives the repeated response that she is a bother. This reinforces the primary schizoid experience. The mother cannot provide for the infant because of a combination of factors, including her own emotional deprivation, the feeling that she has no love to give, the marital and environmental problems in her life, and her clinical depression. As Winnicott (1960) states, for the caregiver to be able to experience the primary maternal preoccupation that the infant needs, there must be a supportive, holding environment for the mother. Thus, the infant is right to feel that she does not love enough but is unaware of all the factors. Given the infant's egocentric cognitive capacity, he cannot but feel that he is unloved because he is worthless and his love is bad, the same as when he is loved he feels it is because he is worthwhile and his love is good. The infant cannot know of the multiple factors that can contribute to the object not being able to love him, which do not have to do with the infant but rather with deficiencies in the caregiver's personality, environment, and the like.

SUGGESTIONS IN TECHNIQUE

It will be noted that on occasion I brought myself directly into the interventions, for instance by stating to Annette that I wanted her to be alive and not a dead person. Annette was developmentally unable to go on being for herself. Ideally, it would have been preferable if she could be a live person for herself. At this point, it was crucial for her to be alive and therefore I used myself directly in the intervention so that she could begin to use me as a potentially good object. Eventually, she will need to differentiate and be a live person for herself and not for the object. A case discussion in the last chapter will illustrate this process.

It is important for the therapist to help the patient to become aware of those aspects of parenting that interfered with his development. At the same time, the therapist also helps the patient to see that his infantile state at the time could have influenced his interpretation of events. The internal bad object is often more terrible and awe-inspiring than its external counterpart (Seinfeld 1990). As the patient becomes aware of the actual failures in parenting that contributed to his developmental schizoid problems, he often becomes angry at his parents. One patient wondered what to do with his rage toward them in the present. He had little contact with them. Their current behavior was no longer influential. The therapist pointed out that what it was necessary to change was the parental inner influence. He could see that it would not do him or his parents much good to address the past. As the patient becomes able to understand that others have a subjective life, the therapist might interpret that parents also have their own subjective issues, including those from their own childhood.

The therapist may sometimes help the patient reconstruct the past relationships with parents from current events. For instance, one adult patient had moved to New York, and when his parents visited, they said discouragingly, "You are not going to stay in New York forever?" The patient was able to begin to see that his parents had always discouraged his confidence in activities that were the outcome of his own autonomous needs and not oriented toward fulfilling their needs. Another patient visited home and his parents wanted him to sleep in his sister's old room. This reminded him that they preferred his sister because she had remained dependent, and they communicated that they wanted him to be dependent.

In the treatment of schizoid individuals, it is important that the therapist confront the internal parental influences as soon as these are recognized. At the same time, the therapist helps the patient preserve whatever positive images he has of parental figures so as not to be overwhelmed by an objectless state. The therapist must sometimes be vigorous in pointing out the internal negative parental influence. One patient was cruelly self-critical about small mistakes she had made at work. She then feared her bosses would punish her even though there was no evidence that they shared her view of herself. The therapist and the patient had previously discussed her mother's harsh criticism. Thus the therapist directly interpreted the self-torture as emanating from the internal mother and the patient's fear of the boss as a projection of the internal mother. The patient professed to understanding but then went off to criticize herself harshly for other minor matters. The therapist had to point out how she was again manifesting the inner cruel parental influence. The patient laughed, saying she couldn't seem to stop herself. The therapist explored her fear of quieting the voice in her mind she had always known, and thus losing a long-standing "relationship." The patient might need to hold onto a negative inner relationship because to give it up might threaten her with an objectless state. With such cases, the therapist should not continue to confront the patient but instead empathize with the fear of loss and allow for the patient to gradually internalize the therapist as a good object. The patient cannot risk the loss of the negative introjects until there is a secure-enough internal good object to replace them with.

The schizoid patient will often talk for a prolonged period about outside interests, events, or persons and not talk directly about himself. One patient discussed her husband, children, and colleagues at work. She laughingly said we psychoanalyzed everyone but her. In such a case, the objects discussed serve a function similar to the use of board games in child therapy, providing the dyad with a nonthreatening transitional object through which to relate. Only after a period of such playing, sometimes lasting years, should the therapist endeavor to interpret the meaning of the verbal play.

There are other, more severely disturbed schizoid patients whose discussions of outside people and events take a more troublesome course. One middle-aged woman concentrated upon her difficulties with her husband and adult children in ways where she could have no beneficial effect. She would complain that a daughter living independently was unmarried. She disapproved of the woman her son lived with. She complained of another daughter's choice of career. She described her own relationship to her husband as "ideal," but she disapproved of the ways in which he related to other persons. She would become depressed, suicidal, and enraged about these circumstances that she could not change. She complained that therapy was useless because it could not change her life. If I responded with understanding for the disappointment she felt, she became more depressed and enraged and felt justified in her reaction. I interpreted the current disappointments as displacements in relationships, and she described persons she had lost or who disappointed her throughout her adolescence and adult life. She would not explore her childhood, insisting that her mother was an angel and her father was a gruff, ignorant man, and there was nothing further to say. In the countertransference, I felt both helpless and angry in that she presented herself as suffering and suicidal but would only focus on problems that we could not effect therapeutically. I finally confronted her that she continually focused on these other persons to escape from herself and that the purpose of therapy was for us to focus on her, her inner life, and the reason for her feelings. She replied,

"How can I focus on myself when I know my children are suffering?"

I questioned whether they suffered and also whether she believed she should suffer because she thought they suffered. She mentioned the unmarried daughter as one who suffered in her loneliness. I reminded her of remarks she had made that indicated that there were positive aspects to the daughter's life, and that she might not suffer as the mother imagined. I said, "You imagine her as suffering, but that is still you playing at being her so it is your suffering you are describing." I then follow up this statement with an objective inquiry as to what the daughter actually said, how she behaved, what was happening in her life, and so forth, which the mother based her fantasies upon. The patient replied that her daughter says she is happy, talks about her job with excitement, but there have been occasions when the mother found her to be lonely or depressed. I responded that we cannot be sure of what is happening with the daughter in reality but that the mother might picture her as suffering because of the mother's own feelings of how terrible it would be to be alone with herself.

I then said that even if the daughter were suffering as the mother fantasized, it would not be inevitable that the mother would have to suffer. The daughter is an adult who can do something about her situation, or if she cannot, she can go for treatment, and the mother is suffering for her own reasons, not for the daughter, since the suffering does not help the daughter. In each session, as the patient suffered over someone, I reiterated that she was not suffering for the person or to help the person, but to escape from herself into the role of the other.

I continued intervening in this way because I saw the patient responded positively.

At first she complained that I lacked family values, did not believe in altruism, and could never understand her. However, as she protested, she became lively and less depressed. I continued to assert that in treatment we should look at her inner life, explore her family life, and concentrate on her motivations. She finally said she did not know how to focus on herself. She was considering what I was saying, and it was beginning to make sense, but she did not know how to do it.

I interpreted that she always had to think about others, to fill her mind with feelings and concern about others. I said, "Engaging in this therapy poses a problem for us. You are accustomed to feeling for others, what it is you imagine them to feel. You have no experience thinking, feeling, or living for yourself. We can see that this living through others has taken you to the brink of disaster. But now we have reached the point in treatment where you realize therapy is about discovering and expressing your own feelings, thoughts, and motives. But this process is completely foreign to you. Therapy requires that you do exactly what it is you have never known or been able to do."

Until this point, the patient had no idea that there was another way that she could be experiencing and conducting herself in therapy. It never occurred to her that she could focus on herself and not on others. In fact, her only self-awareness was her suffering for others and her wish to change and to control them. The possibility was raised that she could focus on herself instead of on others. If she grasped the possibility and experienced the lack of focusing upon herself, this feeling of lack and sense of possibility would become in itself the beginning of a sense of self, separate from others. The possibility would become an ideal creating an ambition or motivation to focus on herself, that she could strive for. My interventions were aimed at making her aware of the lack of self. Once she felt this lack, she would be able to become the possibility that we have created. Grolnick (1990) states that Winnicott's conception of the self is based on Kierkegaard's idea of the self as becoming. In those patients who experienced privation in ego care in the beginning of life and are therefore deficit in psychic structure, the therapist intervenes by making them aware of what is lacking. The patient thereby experiences a sense of emptiness or lack, which he endeavors to alleviate through becoming whatever it is that he is lacking.

The patient reported feeling despondent at the awareness that she lacked a sense of self and lived through others. For the first time, she began to recall fleeting memories. She stated that in her childhood, her mother had told her that she was such an ugly baby that her mother took her through the back streets to avoid being seen by mother's acquaintances. The patient wondered what this incident might mean about her mother, her mother's feelings about her, her development, and self-image. She began to think about herself and to report various problems and patterns. She suffered from migraines. She did not like to eat. She went through intervals of avoiding food or vomiting what she ate. She recalled fleeting memories of unpleasant incidents with her family in childhood. In this way she began to develop and focus upon her self in the treatment.

Klein (1935) defined the depressive position in terms of the child's concern and guilt over aggressively injuring internal good objects. The patient's suffering for her children and her husband appears to be the result of an ego fixation in the depressive position in that her suffering over an injured object could reflect an unconscious phantasy that she has aggressively injured the good object and now must atone. However, the fact that the self is nearly nonexistent if it is not living through the object suggests a fundamental ego fixation at the level of the earlier schizoid fixation. Thus, the patient uses the object relations of the depressive position characterized by aggression, guilt, and atonement to compensate for the deficiencies of the self associated with the schizoid position.

THE SCHIZOID FEAR OF ENGULFMENT

The schizoid patient's deficiencies of the self may also be manifest in severe anxiety about being engulfed by the therapist's mirroring responses. In the treatment of these patients, the therapist should only join the patient in the sharing of his interest in the transitional object or his other-than-human interests and not interpret its meaning to the patient on any level. For instance, a patient might come into therapy speaking of a newfound interest in making collages. The therapist might comment that the pasting together of fragments represents the patient's efforts of achieving a cohesive self. This intervention, highly supportive of the self in the treatment of the narcissistic personality, may be objectifying for the schizoid personality. If the therapist prematurely interprets the striving for unity, the patient may feel that the therapist steals the striving from him and transforms it into something for the therapist instead of for the patient. For some time, the therapist may have to relate to the patient only about the activity in itself with no reference to extenuating meaning.

Winnicott (1971) has discussed the importance of the therapist's tolerating the patient's playing without attributing higher meaning or purpose to the play. The therapist thereby allows the patient to find his personal meaning. When the patient talks about external matters without attributing meanings to them, the therapist may feel that this is "nonsense" or that the session is chaotic and without purpose. There is often therapeutic value to tolerating nonsense, chaos, purposelessness. The patient is beginning to psychically handle and play with the objects discussed. In response to the patient, the therapist must be genuinely interested and enthusiastic.

Intervening in the Patient's Dread of Engulfment

When the patient's life is chaotic, that is, changing jobs, relationships, homes, the therapist empathically understands the patient's world view and acknowledges explicitly the real, alienating, and engulfing aspects of daily life. Some schizoid patients may be more successful in relationships and obtaining job security if the therapist supports and actively helps the effort to preserve autonomy instead of pressuring them to become involved prematurely. As patients successfully preserve autonomy, they become less fearful of involvement. One patient began to create distance from an intrusive mother by lying to her about his plans and avoiding her whenever possible. The therapist did not pressure him to deal with the mother more directly. Lying was the only way he could, at this point, evade her prying. In his childhood, the patient had never lied because he believed that his mother could read his mind. He had been warned that he better not lie because mother would certainly know. When he did not give in to his mother's demands to visit at her beck and call, but instead lied and said he had important plans, the therapist remarked on his efforts at autonomy and the growing sense that his mother could not read his mind. The therapist did not question why he lied and was not direct in focusing on his fear of self-assertion. In the treatment of the schizoid, the therapist must give considerable attention to what small steps in improvement are an expression of the patient's full capacity. It could be quite destructive to demand that the schizoid encounter tasks beyond his emotional capabilities.

The therapist cannot confront the patient's fear of involvement in relationships, work, or the demands of living so long as the patient is primarily concerned with avoiding engulfment by the object. Premature interventions about the patient's fear of closeness and commitment cannot be utilized by the patient. It is only after the therapist helps the patient to maintain a degree of autonomy that the patient will be less fearful and motivated to involve himself in relationships, work commitments, and stable living. It is at this point that the therapist vigorously confronts and interprets the patient's anxieties, fears, and resistances.

One patient playfully lived by taking an apartment, paying the rent, discontinuing paying the rent, then fleeing to another abode. The therapist did not confront her with her acting out. During the first few years of treatment the therapist demonstrated the patient's lack of an internal good relationship resulting in ego deficits such as capacity for positive expectations, impulse control, and frustration tolerance. Meanwhile, the therapist empathically responded to her statements that work was imprisoning and that she resented giving up her money to landlords who do not do anything for it. As she increasingly internalized a positive object relationship, she felt more vulnerable about her precarious life and became motivated for stability and security. She decided she would have to work steadily and pay the rent. For the first year she kept to her plan. In one session she came into therapy angrily describing how she had stopped paying her rent temporarily because she was behind in bills. She had received an eviction notice. She was panicked because she did not want to move and return to her previous life pattern. However, as she continued to talk she angrily identified various problems in the apartment that the landlord had never fixed and how he did not deserve the rent because he was not a good landlord and she was asserting her tenant's rights. Her tone had dramatically changed from guilt to self-righteousness and indignation. At this point I confronted the fact that she had at first made no mention of withholding of rent as a social protest nor had she taken any of the appropriate legal steps. I confronted her with an avoidance of her guilt and responsibility and the wish not to pay her way by proclaiming and fantasizing that she was an oppressed tenant taking a social action. She was then able to acknowledge that she spent the rent money on clothes, entertainment, and so forth.

The patient's current actions were not so much based on a fear of engulfment but rather on the wish to be taken care of and loved. Winnicott (1956) states that antisocial conduct is often a displacement of protest concerning deprivation in early life. This patient's withholding of the rent money and purchases of clothes and entertainment are symbolic expressions of her infantile protest that she had a right to nurturance, ego care, and love. Stealing is therefore an expression of this early right to be loved. The therapist must first confront the displacement and self-justifications, thereby allowing the patient to realize the infantile nature of the antisocial act. It is only at this point that the therapist can effectively empathize with the patient as a child experiencing deprivation and, therefore, "stealing" the love she is entitled to. If I empathized with this patient in her feeling entitled to withhold the rent because her apartment was not repaired, when she did not take any of the appropriate legal actions and impulsively spent the rent money, I would only have reinforced her antisocial behavior.

As the fear of engulfment receded, the infantile longing to be loved in the transference was emerging. She expressed this only indirectly, in the greed for material things and the wish to be taken care of for free. She began to report to work late, take days off, extend her lunch hour, and then was indignant when the boss confronted her. I remarked that her need for love was also disguisedly expressed at work in the wish that the boss would provide her with special treatment, allowing her to break the rules and regulations. When the boss became angry, she became even more rebellious. She had been viciously abused as a child by both parents. The abuse was the only attention she received from them. In her need for love, she was transforming the boss into the abusive parent. Her behavior now at work differed from her former behavior when she had been primarily concerned with the fear of engulfment. At that time, she had not continued to provoke the boss with an infraction of the rules, but rather she quit the job after the first complaints. Thus, I interpreted that she was now beginning to want love as she became less afraid of engulfment. I said, "You are trying to transform your boss into the ass-kicking parent because you are becoming hungry for love and attention. You do not know how to ask for attention except in the familiar way you have always known, the experience of ass-kicking. This is at least some form of contact, this abusive pattern, but it also closes off the possibility of a more positive contact, which you fear."

Unlike the borderline patient, the schizoid individual is not *primarily* concerned that he will be abandoned for his newfound autonomy (although this could be a factor) but rather he is in panic about being abandoned for his need for love, which begins to emerge as he becomes less fearful of engulfment.

INTERPRETING THE EMPTY CORE

The patient may manifest a need for love in the substitutive need for food, drugs, alcohol, or persons. The therapist directly interprets the destructive emotions of greed, envy, and sadism. He explains that the patient found a natural need for love became an all-consuming, destructive greed. The patient therefore had to repress these feelings, which then grew in strength. If the need for love and care are not met, greed, envy, and a strong inclination to injure the unresponsive object may follow and be structured in the psyche. The therapist then explains that the patient has shifted the need for humans, which he cannot control, to a need for "things," which can be controlled. There is also the effort to transform humans into things in domineering, controlling relationships.

The therapist focuses especially on transference interpretation. Thus, if the patient begins to be dominant in relationships in the course of the treatment, the therapist should explore whether this behavior is not a displacement of the transference. The therapist explores whether the patient has

not been subtly disappointed and deprived and is feeling that
he cannot depend upon the reliability of the therapist, and
therefore is trying to omnipotently control other persons as he
wishes he could control the therapist. The patient's becoming
addicted or excessively needy of nonhuman activities or objects may also be explored as transference displacements.

Borderline patients are liable to protest loudly and express overt dependence, loss, and anger at the time of the
therapist's vacation, holidays, or minor disruptions. The
schizoid patient usually denies any reaction to the therapist's
vacation or other separations. Thus, when the therapist an-
nounces the vacation, the patient is likely to say "It's no
problem. I'll save money. I don't know why you keep
bringing it up. You're entitled to go away. It's only a few
weeks. I'll live."

One patient responded this way but the session before I
was to leave he did not show or call to cancel. I called him and
he was surprised to hear from me saying, "I thought you left
already. I did not realize we had another session before you
were leaving. I mixed it up."

The patient might also forget the appointment on the
date the therapist returns. The patient's forgetting expresses
both the denial of the therapist's importance to him as well as
his unconscious anger. It is important for the therapist to
continually and actively discuss impending vacations or holidays despite the patient's protest that he is unaffected. The
therapist may reduce the risk of the patient acting out resistances by repeatedly raising the issue of the disruption.

In general, the therapist should directly interpret all manifestations of negative transference. Because the patient avoids
libidinal attachment, there is not a strong positive transference
to counteract negative therapeutic reactions. Therefore, the
schizoid is at risk to drop out of therapy prematurely if he is
disappointed or angry. The therapist is also faced with the
dilemma that the patient is extremely sensitive to rejections

but rarely acknowledges, even to himself, that he feels rejected. If the therapist disappoints the patient, for instance, by arriving late for a session, the schizoid patient is not likely to complain. If the therapist raised the issue, the patient is likely to say that it is not a problem, anyone can be late, he doesn't take such things personally. However, in the session he may be more withdrawn or come late the next session, or complain about other persons who do not care about him. The therapist must actively listen to any evidence of a negative reaction by the patient and draw the connection to his attention. The therapist should also overtly insist on the patient's right to his reaction from his own subjective point of view. The schizoid patient is sometimes extremely objective in his response to the therapist. Thus he readily expresses an objective understanding of disappointments in the therapist. He understands that the therapist does not reject him personally but instead acts for reasons for his own. However, as Little (1986) points out, the schizoid's objectivity is often of a pseudo nature and serves to defend against a delusional transference. Thus, the patient may cognitively understand the objective reasons that the therapist goes away on vacation but his actions may express a strong subjective reaction and feelings of rejection. The schizoid is at risk to quit therapy prematurely if the therapist does not help him to verbalize negative reactions.

8

TREATMENT OF SCHIZOID STATES IN CHILDREN

MELANIE KLEIN AND PERSONIFICATION IN PLAY THERAPY

Klein originated the play technique in the treatment of children. She discovered that the child's play was equivalent to the adult's free associations and dreams in serving as the royal road to the unconscious. In her paper "The Psychological Principles of Early Analysis" (1926), Klein suggested that the play content of children was identical to the nucleus of masturbation fantasies and served as an outlet for discharge. In "Personification in the Play of Children" (1929), she broadened her concept of play by suggesting that it served as a representation of general unconscious wish fulfillment. The dreams, spirits, ghosts, fairies, angels, and devils of the child's inner fantasy world were personified in his play. Thus, the child enacted the drama of his internal object world in his play with puppets, dolls, figurines, toy soldiers, and so forth. The child also enacted internalized object relations in role-playing.

Klein (1929) discussed the case of Erma, a 6-year-old youngster, who identified with the sadistic bad object by torturing and abusing the therapist, who assumed the role of the child. In play therapy, the strengthening of the internal good object may be manifested in the increasing appearances of rescuers or saviors who protect the victim from the bad object. The child might obscure his identification with a sadistic bad object by designating the enemy all-bad and thereby morally justifying punitive rageful retaliation. A child who regularly played toy soldiers with the therapist insisted that his army were "the good guys" threatened by the therapist's evil soldiers. The extent of the torture and annihilation of the enemy after the battle had been won revealed the child's identification with the bad object.

THE SCHIZOID CHILD'S INCAPACITY TO SYMBOLIZE

In "The Importance of Symbol-Formation in the Development of the Ego" (1930), Klein pointed out that a central problem of the schizoid youngster is his incapacity to symbolize or to play in the proper sense. She states:

> They perform certain monotonous actions, and it is a laborious piece of work to penetrate from these to the unconscious. When we do succeed, we find that the wish fulfillment associated with these actions is preeminently the negation of reality and the inhibition of phantasy. In these extreme cases personification does not succeed." [p. 199]

Klein points out that it is the child's capacity for symbol formation that is the maturational foundation of the personification of fantasy in play. The infant's sadism toward the object is the bedrock of symbol formation. Klein states that the infant's wish to destroy the part object of breast, phallus, and vagina gives rise to a dread of retaliation. The child copes with his anxiety by substituting innocuous objects for the dreaded part objects. Thus, the child has the materials and objects in his everyday world represent the feared part objects. The child will feel toward the replacement the same dread he had felt for the original part object, but through play he will strive for mastery of anxiety.

A youngster had seen a Stephen King film about a demonic automobile named Christine. In session he played Christine with a tiny model car. He was in control of the furious, omnipotent car and turned it on his enemies. In the Kleinian view, the car represents the omniscient dreaded breast/phallus. He mastered his anxiety by transforming the part object into the car that he could control. Further symbol formation occurred through the bad object being further divided and symbolized in the enemies that "Christine" destroyed. Through symbol formation, the youngster manages the anxiety related to the wish to enter into mother's body and steal its contents (breast, phallus, feces, and baby). According to the Kleinian model, the child neutralizes the retaliatory contents by transforming them into less malevolent symbols and representations. Klein says: "Thus, not only does symbolism come to be the foundation of all phantasy and sublimation but, more than that, it is the subject's relation to the outside world and to reality in general" (p. 221).

THE CASE OF DICK AND THE INCAPACITY IN SYMBOL FORMATION

The Problem

Dick is a 4-year-old whom Klein presented to illustrate the pathological incapacity for symbol formation. He had achieved a vocabulary and intellectual capacity of a child around 15 to 18 months old. He was indifferent to his mother and nurse, and he had not adapted to his environment or reality. He lacked affect, was impoverished, and presented anxiety with an extreme oppositional attitude. He expressed little desire for comfort or love and diminished sensibility for pain. This symptomology coupled with the absence of hallucinations or delusions, suggested a diagnosis of schizoid personality.

In the beginning of treatment, Dick left his nurse without anxiety. In the session he ran circles around Klein as if she were a piece of the furniture. He stared distractedly into space with no interest in the objects at hand. Klein astutely compared him to the severely neurotic child who might subtly approach the play materials only to quickly turn away. Dick did not show these signs of latent anxiety.

History

Klein reports that Dick neglected the breast and nearly starved to death in the first months of life. (The reader will recall Ellen West's rejection of breast, later of milk, and finally of all food. Anorexia in the first months of life is common in schizoid patients). Dick had an equally difficult time later with a wet nurse and with the introduction of solid foods. Klein states that although his physical needs were well attended, he did not receive love from either his mother, father, or the original nurse. At around the age of two, Dick had a new nurse who showed him love and handled him affectionately. He also had more contact with a grandmother who was fond of him. There was a definite response to the improved care: Dick was toilet trained shortly thereafter and became less of a fussy eater. He improved his rote learning. Despite these gains, Dick remained, for the most part, unrelated to the nurse and grandmother. His fundamental deficiencies remained unaltered. Klein believed that Dick suffered deficits in the constitutional capacity of the ego to tolerate anxiety and in the love and nurturance he received from his family. She states:

> The genital had begun to play its part very early; this caused a premature and exaggerated identification with the object attacked and had contributed to an equally premature defense against sadism. The ego had ceased to develop phantasy-life and to establish a relation with reality after a feeble beginning, symbol formation in this child had come to a standstill." [p. 224]

Treatment

Dick was indifferent to most persons and objects except for doors, door handles, and the opening and shutting of doors. In the analysis, the major obstacles to be surmounted were Dick's defective speech and his incapacity to symbolize. In early sessions Dick showed no interest in the toys or play material. Klein pointed toward two trains, a large one and a small one. Klein named them a Daddy Train and a Dick Train. He picked up the Dick Train and rolled in to the window, naming it "Station." Klein interpreted that Dick was going inside of his Mommy. He dropped the train and raced in a space between the inner and outer doors, shutting himself in and crying "Dar," then emerging again. Melanie Klein commented that Dick was inside the Dark Mommy.

Lacan and Klein's Case of Dick

In his seminars on technique, Lacan (1988) discusses Klein's treatment of Dick.

Lacan says:

> So what did Melanie Klein actually do?—Nothing other
> than to bring in verbalization. She symbolized an effective
> relationship, that of one named being with another. She
> plastered on the symbolization of the oedipal myth, to give
> it its real name. It's from that point on that, after an initial
> ceremony, taking refuge in the dark in order to renew
> contact with the container, something new awakens in the
> child." [p. 86]

Lacan remarks that Klein's direct interpretations result in the child verbalizing his first spoken call—he asks Klein for his nurse—the person he had arrived with and then had allowed to depart as if she were nothing to him. Lacan points out that Klein humanizes the child by grafting him onto the law of speech. It is not so much a question of whether she is correct in her interpretations but rather that she has introduced Dick into the symbolic order of the oedipal myth through language.

> Things then progress to the point where Melanie Klein
> brings into play all the other elements of a situation which is
> from the organized, oedipal complex, right up to and in-
> cluding, the father himself, who comes to take his own part.
> Outside of the sessions, Melanie Klein says, the child's
> relations unfold on the plane of the oedipus complex. The
> child symbolizes the reality around him starting from this
> nucleus, the little palpitating cell of symbolism which Me-
> lanie Klein gave him. [p. 85]

Lacan also notes that when the call (for the nurse) is first made, dependency relations establish themselves. Hence-forth, Dick will welcome his nurse with open arms, and in hiding behind the door, reveal the need to have Melanie Klein join him in this cramped, close quarter. As Lacan stated:

"Dependency will come in its train" (p. 87). Lacan is describing how the child develops a subjective sense of I under the watchful eye of Melanie Klein. She is painting a picture of Dick being in the oedipal phase and names him the phallus. He in turn is internalizing this identity: a phallus being in the oedipal phase of development. It seems that the danger in this work is that Dick may be internalizing a false self based upon Melanie Klein's image of him being in the world. He is becoming Melanie Klein's Dick. His escape behind the door, calling for his nurse, may have been his last-ditch effort to escape the watchful, objectifying eye of Melanie Klein. Given the empty core of the schizoid child, it is no wonder that he can take on a ready-made oedipal suit of identity.

The following clinical vignette based on the treatment of a prepubertal child will illustrate some treatment issues in work with schizoid children.

THE CASE OF MARY

Mary, a 9-year-old, was referred for treatment by the special school for emotionally disturbed youngsters she attended. Mary was described by the school as unrelated to teachers and peers, and apathetic about homework, alternating between being withdrawn or hyperactive and destructive.

Mary came from a chaotic, multiple-problem family and was the third of seven siblings. The mother had a history of psychiatric hospitalization and was diagnosed as being subject to schizophrenic episodes. Some of the children had been removed from the home on various occasions because they had been found to be abused or neglected. The mother was a single parent. Her live-in boyfriend ignored the children except to hit them if they disturbed him. The children were needy and competed for limited oral supplies. The mother appeared uninvolved with their needs and overburdened by environmental stress and her emotional problems. She had on occasion abused the children, being unable to manage them.

The mother could provide no specific developmental information about Mary and seemed not to have a clear picture of her, distinct from the other children. The siblings nicknamed Mary "Cloud Nine" because she lived in her own world.

Treatment

In the initial sessions with Mary, I attempted to engage her in what I thought were nonthreatening discussions of bare essentials concerning who I was, who she was, what we do together. She did not respond intelligibly but made silly facial expressions and animallike sounds. The puppets, dolls, and toys in my office did not seem to appeal to her for their use in symbolic play. She examined the toys with little interest, tested if they could be pulled apart and then sat in a little chair, rocking and fiddling with a rubber band, stretching, rolling, wrapping it around her finger, hand, wrist, putting it into her mouth, removing it, and spreading her saliva so that it covered its length. During the early sessions she handled various items. For instance, she took a plain sheet of paper, rolled, squashed, pressed, spread it out and followed the wrinkles with her finger that had been produced.

While she handled the material in the office, I stood around watching and not saying anything. Mary's nose was running and she took a tissue from the Kleenex box. She wiped her nose and dropped the tissue on the floor. She glanced over at me and then dropped paper on the floor, then a pencil, and then the play materials. She then dropped to her knees, handled the materials, and began to stick them into her mouth. I commented, "The things dropped. Lost. In your mouth, back inside of you and now they are not lost."

She gave me a big smile, making eye contact for the first time. She began ravenously to put the materials into her mouth or press them against her body, then she laughed and spit them out. I understood she was playing at losing parts of herself, such as feces, and then denying the loss by placing those parts back inside. I said, "Things dropped," and not "She dropped things" followed by "loss" to focus upon the signifier of her anxiety. I thought that her stuffing of herself right after my intervention reflected that I had identified the source of her anxiety. She was then able to let the things go.

In subsequent sessions she exhibited further strange behavior. She would come into sessions and begin to contort her body by twisting an arm behind her back, stretching a leg over head, bowing and twisting her head over her shoulder. She groaned and grunted as if in pain. I watched, then asked what was happening. She did not respond. Another time when I looked over at her, she said "wrestling." She alluded to John doing something to Joey, Mary doing something to Tina, John doing something to Mary. I realized that she was demonstrating how she and her siblings wrestled or how they observed wrestling on television. At intervals between wrestling, she would pull on a rubber band, stretching it to the limit. Once it broke and she became quite upset. I assured her that she had not done anything wrong, that I was not upset, but this had nothing to do with her response. When she stretched the rubber band again she was careful not to break it. She then twisted herself in what seemed to be a wrestling hold, and I had the thought that she looked stretched out in the same way that the rubber band had been. I remarked "Nothing is broken. Mary is all together." When she twisted her arm I said, "The arm doesn't come off." When she twisted her head, I'd remark, "The head doesn't come off," and so on. She began to join me by saying, as she pulled on a puppet on my desk, "The arm doesn't come off." I understood her actions not to relate primarily to castration anxiety but rather to a fragmented self. Through her contortions she began to see that she was not disjointed or fragmented. Thus, she was experiencing a sense of her own boundedness and wholeness, maybe in the manner of what Thomas Ogden (1989) has conceptualized as the sensory-dominated mode of structuring experience referred to as "the autistic-contiguous position" (p. 81).

I now intervened by mirroring her behavior. I handled materials, stretching them without breaking them, pulling at limbs and arms and emphasizing, with Chaplinesque exaggeration, that everything was still together and whole. She laughed with recognition at the mirroring and now, in her own playacting, stressed the unity of the object, showing me that it was whole.

When she contorted herself into wrestling holds, I commented "Mary is in a hold," and then "Mary is being held." At one point, she wrapped her arms around herself and said, "I hug me." She also flung herself onto the floor and rolled around on the rug and asked me to roll her. It is possible that she also experienced a sense of boundedness in feeling the friction of her skin pressed against the floor.

Mary was a chronic, compulsive hand-washer. When anxious in sessions she sometimes rubbed her hands together. I rubbed the palms of my hands together vigorously so that the friction could be heard. I said "friction." She smiled and tried doing the same, saying "friction."

Mary would make animal-like noises and silly faces. She asked me to imitate her noises and to make the same faces. I did. She laughed hysterically. She said, "You look silly" or "crazy" while pointing at my silly facial expression. She would tap on my desk with a pen three times and gesture for me to follow suit. I would begin to tap and then she'd stop me. She tapped again. I automatically tapped in response. She tapped twice, I once, she tapped three times, I tapped twice, she tapped four times, I tapped three times and on and on until she dropped her pen and I dropped mine. In this way she played at taking the lead, initiating the play and having me respond, serving as a mirror and an echo.

After I had mirrored her, she asked me to close my eyes. When I opened them she had disappeared. I heard a noise beneath the desk. I did not immediately find her. There was more moving about and shuffling. I looked under the desk. She laughed. Thus, she practiced escaping from her mirroring object, being found, and being mirrored again.

She drew pictures. The first ones had a bright, sunny,

maniclike quality. There were bright golden flowers, a lavish green park, a smiling family of mother and baby. Gradually, aggression appeared in her drawings. The green park was colored over red, reflecting fire. The golden flowers were trampled, cut by large, ugly boots.

In our next session, she brought in a pair of play handcuffs to see if they fit me. I permitted her to handcuff me. She reported that the keys were lost. She said I was in her power and her slave. She kept me in the handcuffs for nearly the entire session. In this way she played out her need for omnipotence. She transformed the Other into an object and herself into a subject.

She continued the subject–object theme throughout our next session in a game of tag. I would catch and tag her. Next she set up a row of chairs for us to turn around. Whenever I nearly caught her, she'd scream and cry, "Stop!" I stopped in my tracks and we resumed the play at her direction. In this way we played out the theme of the engulfing mother, with Mary having the power to petrify me into an object by commanding me to stop. Only after a prolonged period was she able to allow me the freedom to catch her if I could.

Once she no longer needed to control me and could allow me the liberty to play at my own speed, she began to accept the possibility that she and I could both be subjects. The child cannot compete until she is able to cope with the other's subjectivity. Mary's family life was fraught with intrusion and chaos, with a multitude of persons treating her as an object. She needed an extended period during which she could assume a position of an omnipotent subject and place the other into the position of the object.

At first, I mirrored Mary's need for wholeness to gradually establish myself as a mirroring object. She then brought her self to me for mirroring. Lacan (1949) refers to the fragmented infant attempting to find a unitary wholeness in the specular mirror image. The therapist can serve as such a mirror by reflecting to the child his striving for a unitary self-image. Once Mary felt reflected in the therapist's mirroring, she had to escape becoming an object of the therapist, so she became invisible by playing the game of hide-and-go-seek. This disappearance results in a sense of loss of self. Mary dealt with this feeling with a manic defense, then in her drawings. The manic defense broke down into the image of the fragmented self as manifested in the destruction of the park and flowers in her pictures. She therefore again sought the therapist as an object, at first needing to omnipotently control him but gradually permitting him to come to life and liberty as a human object.

It will be noted that although Mary was an extremely deprived child, her play did not reflect being emotionally deprived by her mother. Rather the play showed the fleeing from an engulfing object. I had helped her use me as a mirroring object to protect her from fragmentation. In the period of Mary's omnipotent control over the engulfing therapist, she rolled on the rug hysterically, sucking at her fingers, pretending to put her toes into her mouth. I said, "You are feeling like a contented baby with everything you could possibly need, playing with your fingers and toes. Mary became more regressed and silly in response to the therapist, saying, "Mary is a little baby playing with her fingers and toes." She would continue these actions that resembled a contented baby. I did not necessarily interpret these actions. Sometimes I said nothing, which allowed her to play the regressive part.

A while later, I made the interpretation in response to the regressive, manic behavior, "Mary is playing at being a contented, happy baby, sucking at her thumbs and toes, a baby who has everything and needs nothing, not even a Mommy." Mary became agitated. She began to play distractedly, more hyperactively. She demanded cookies. I provided her with some, which she ate ravenously. She insisted on more cookies. I said, "Mary wants to fill herself up on cookies so she doesn't need anything and can be a perfectly happy baby again." I made this comment a number of times in response to Mary's demanding hyperactivity.

At one point, after I interpreted her manic denial of need, she went under the desk. I remarked that Mary wanted to be invisible, she did not want to be seen by me because I say things about her she does not like. She would then at times spontaneously acknowledge the wish to be invisible. It should be emphasized that I did not interpret the manic defense against object loss immediately. I waited a prolonged period, nearly a year of twice-weekly treatment, until she had sufficiently established me as an object and showed signs of tolerating my subjectivity. These interpretations could only be made after she had shown some capacity to tolerate me as a subject and after there had been a sufficient degree of corrective experience in relation to her feeling intruded upon by the object, by allowing her some control with the object.

On occasion I met with Mary and her mother to provide guidance and to see their interaction. The mother did not relate well to Mary, talking about her as if she was not there. While discussing their difficulties, she often smiled when the topic should have evoked tears. I noticed a new aspect of Mary's communication pattern. Mary spoke to her mother in a soft, hesitant, mumbling, barely audible voice. Her hesitation in speaking was not only directed to the mother, but was part of all of her communications. I checked with her special school and was informed that she had a full language and speech evaluation. There was no organicity and it was thought that her quiet and hesitant speech related to a poor self-image.

When I questioned her or when speaking spontaneously, I noted again that she could hardly be heard. In previous sessions, I attended so closely to her nonverbal communication that I had not given much thought to her speech. Only in play did she call out vigorously. It was as if she forgot herself. In one session, when she mumbled hesitantly I asked again what she wanted. She pointed to the play dough. I handed it to her. I then said, "Mary speaks so quietly, maybe she is afraid to ask me for something."

I developed this style of speaking about her in the third person because it proved to be the only way she responded. If I referred to her directly she turned away. On this occasion, she did not respond even though I called her Mary. At other times, I continued to remark, "Mary thinks she is not supposed to speak loud; Mary thinks she should not be heard; Mary thinks if she speaks loudly, she bothers me; Mary thinks she shouldn't ask me for anything or she'll bother me; Mary thinks I don't want to be bothered."

These remarks were made in a number of interviews so as not to overwhelm her. One day she spontaneously but belatedly responded by saying, "Mary is being quiet. Mary doesn't talk. Everyone says she annoys them."

She looked at me smiling, as if playfully communicating. Not long after, she said her teacher yells at her and her mother strikes her if she bothers her. She continually mentioned the bad teacher she could not bother. I commented that Mary felt she could not bother the therapist or teacher. I said Mary felt the therapist was dead tired and Mary thought the therapist and teacher wanted her to be seen and not heard. I sang that little children should be seen and not heard, playfully.

Mary now began to instruct me to be seen and not heard. I replied that Mary wants the therapist to be seen and not heard and I sat quietly. Mary asked for us to play "store." This was the first time she engaged in symbolic play in the session. She said that in school, the children had done some sort of make-believe store project that week. I tried to reality-test and Mary became annoyed and said I should not bother her. I said, "Mary does not like to be bothered. Mary wants me to be quiet."

In playing at store, I was designated the customer, she the grocer. I was to ask for foods. Whatever I asked for, she did not have. She said I was a pest. She said I wanted too much. She directed that we exchange roles. She asked me for food. I provided her with whatever she requested. She demanded more and more food. There was not enough. She had me sit in the corner perfectly still. Then she directed me to stand. I was not to move and be stiff as a board. She demonstrated how to stand stiffly. I was never stiff enough. If I moved, she scolded me. She wanted me to have her stand stiffly, to inspect if it was stiff enough. I gradually began to interpret. First I said stiff bodies. Then I said something like stiff, dead bodies. I didn't say this in a full sentence, just the words themselves. They quickly caught on with Mary. She now would order me to become a stiff, dead body, especially if she perceived of me bothering her. She called me a child, a naughty child; I bothered everyone; I should stand like a stiff, dead body. Since she sounded like a parent, I said, "Mommy wants her child not to bother her and to be a stiff, dead body." She laughed so hard she rolled on the floor. She became wild, throwing materials about. She kept saying Mommy wants baby to be a stiff, dead baby. Mommy wants baby not to bother her. As she wildly wrecked the office, I said, "Mary is refusing to be a stiff, dead, body. Mary is protesting. Mary is fighting."

After we had fully played out the "dead baby" game, I told Mary that I did not want her to be a dead baby, I wanted her to be a lively, healthy girl. Over the years, I gradually explained to Mary that her mother was worn out, tired, and disturbed and sometimes wanted Mary to be still because of her own problems. Mary once replied that her mother wanted her to be quiet, like a doll. On occasion, she brought a doll into session and poured love over it. She would then fling the doll about, smashing it. I remarked that Mary must feel like that when her mother sometimes threw her around; she treated her like a doll that could not be hurt, and that wasn't human. Once I said Mary must have felt her mother could only give her love if she was still, quiet like a doll, and not alive. There was also this issue that Mary found her mother to be a lifeless doll when she could not provide love, but I never thought to interpret this issue.

I was provided with a vivid example of Mary's love and loyalty for her mother. Out in the waiting room, Mary had become hysterical for no apparent reason. I took her into my office and she told me that her mother had no money, no food, no way to pay the rent. She cried, pleading with me to help. I could not calm her until I made the unequivocal statement that I would help her mother. Before this incident, it was not clear how deep the tie to her mother was because of how she related. I was taken aback even though my theory informed me. I had treated Mary for a number of years previously. She was the first child I saw come alive in the treatment process. Through this case I first understood this theme of the schizoid becoming a dead baby to win the mother's love. Guntrip (1969) posited a final split-off self that he referred to as regressed ego. I believe that Guntrip did not get the full picture; it is his regressed, withdrawn passive ego that I posit to be the patient's personified dead infantile self. The therapeutic task is to reach it and demonstrate that it can be cared for in coming alive.

There is an important technique effective in the treatment of schizoids. Earlier I mentioned that I intervened with Mary by referring to her in the third person. This verbally creates a picture for the child of being and doing. If Mary approaches a toy and hesitates, looking at it, I might say, "Mary looking at the toy," then, "Mary touching the toy." At first I do *not* comment on the child's inner life. If she is schizoid, I do not say "Mary is afraid to touch the toy."

If I made such interventions prematurely, Mary might feel I am a witch who reads her mind. If it is clear Mary hesitates before the toy, I might say, "Mary hesitates before the toy," because this remark does not go too far. This technique is useful in providing a child with verbal mirroring without the therapist actively capturing the child in the mirror by seeing too much or seeing what is not there. The child begins to see himself in the reflection of the therapist's verbal mirror and thereby adopts a point of view about himself. This technique may be considered as helping a child who lives in action develop an "observing ego." Sooner or later, the child, finding himself reflected in the therapist's mirror, will have to escape. He will disappear, become invisible, perhaps play hide-and-go-seek. Winnicott stated that within every individual there is a part of the self that must remain private, unfound, and that must never be reached. Humans need solitude as well as relatedness. In the treatment of the schizoid, the therapist helps the patient to become better able to relate. The therapist must also never forget the need for solitude.

9

APATHY, LOVE, AND HATE IN THE COUNTER-TRANSFERENCE

A primary therapeutic problem in the treatment of the borderline patient is hate in the countertransference (Winnicott 1947). In the treatment of the schizoid patient, a central problem is not only hate, but also apathy in the transference-countertransference. For prolonged periods the patient and therapist may go through the motions of doing therapy and the therapist may experience apathy. Grotstein (1985) states that in defensive projective identification, the patient experiences the unconscious phantasy that unwanted split-off aspects of the self or object have been translocated into the external object often to control or disappear into it. The borderline patient uses projective identification to place the sadistic self or parental image onto the therapist, thereby inducing hate in the countertransference. The schizoid patient uses projective identification to place the neglectful parental image onto the therapist, thereby inducing apathy in the countertransference. The therapist comes to feel as indifferent toward the schizoid patient as the parental object had been. The schizoid patient manifests the same indifference toward

195

the therapist that the parental figure directed toward the patient. This induced lack of empathy on the part of the therapist may be the least addressed countertransference reaction. The countertransference reactions of love, hate, and sexual excitement indicate that the therapist has reactions toward the patient. Although these responses may be uncomfortable, they still may be more acceptable than having no emotional response.

Some common manifestations of countertransference reactions to schizoids include: sleepiness in sessions; a lethargic hypnoticlike state; a loss of memory of the content of preceding sessions; an unusual lack of concern about the patient's well-being; an inability to focus on the patient's material; the sense that either the patient, the therapist, or both are no more alive than the nonhuman objects in the office; the sense that the therapist has become like a vending machine, the patient pays a fee and takes what he needs; the feeling that one is not earning the fee and that the patient is being ripped off; the wish that the patient would miss the next session because the treatment is a waste of time; ideas that the patient is untreatable.

The therapist often feels that the patient is not significantly improving but that a heroic effort to help is not necessary because the patient is not suffering acutely. The patient often anticipates that the therapist does not want to be bothered, that he finds the patient a burden and the patient plans to trouble the therapist as little as possible. The patient communicates in a look, a gesture, or a tone that the therapist should not worry, the patient will not make demands or torture the therapist, and both can put out as little effort as possible to get the job done.

The therapist may feel that the schizoid is not a difficult case but that he is uninteresting. A therapist in a clinic turned away an assignment of a demanding borderline patient but accepted a schizoid patient anticipating that the work would be easier. The therapist's attitude may interfere with the patient's potential progress. It is the therapist's task to help the patient to become a bother. The patient defends against the activation of dependency needs by making himself into an easy, nondemanding patient. As Fairbairn (1940) states, "the schizoid patient fears that his need to love will empty and destroy the object. As the patient's neediness enters the transference, the therapist feels drained."

An adult male patient wrote down his dreams and used the entire session to report on them. After several such sessions he introduced a dream enthusiastically, saying, "This is a really complex one, you will be able to do a lot with it."

The patient provided no associations but looked at the therapist as if expecting to be fed the interpretations. At first, as the patient reported the dreams without affect and unrelated to his life situations, the therapist felt bored and removed. Once the patient stated that he expected the therapist to provide clever feedback, the therapist felt drained.

WHEN APATHY TURNS TO RAGE IN THE COUNTERTRANSFERENCE

The therapist contains the schizoid patient's infantile, worthless, neglected self and object images. After a time, the therapist may experience doubts about his competence and even more disturbingly, may undergo sensory and emotional deprivation in encounters with the patient. Indifference may become transformed into rage. The schizoid patient may have experienced such rage in the relationship with his parents but had no place to direct it. The borderline patient's rage has an outlet in the sadomasochistic, abusive relationship between parent and child. The schizoid patient may have experienced abuse in his early object relationships, but it was often not of a chronic sadomasochistic type but rather of a parent striking out impulsively because the child is experienced as a bother. In the schizoid patient's object relationships, there may be little room for the direct expression of rage, which may be discharged either psychosomatically or in passive-aggressive behavior. The therapist treating a schizoid may find that apathy is transformed into rage, which is acted out in passive-aggressive attitudes and responses. The therapist may become withholding, or late for his sessions, foul up scheduling and hope a different patient appears at the schizoid patient's time. The therapist may take calls in session, fall asleep, select the patient's hour if there is a need to cancel an appointment. The therapist is less likely to react in these passive-aggressive ways with the classic borderline patient if only because the borderline patient would not allow him to get away with it.

CONCRETE AND METAPHORICAL THINKING IN THE SCHIZOID PATIENT

Searles (1962) has discussed the schizophrenic patient's tendency to use concrete thinking as a defense against various repressed emotions. He states that the schizophrenic patient often is unable to distinguish between three classes of objects in the outer world: (1) living but nonhuman things, such as plants and animals, (2) inanimate things, and (3) human beings. Searles describes a psychotic patient who used massive projection not only onto human beings but in addition onto trees, animals, buildings, and a variety of inanimate objects. Thus, the patient expressed his own personality fragmentation by the delusional belief that the building in which he was living might collapse at any moment.

The schizoid patient uses projection to place feelings about his fragile sense of self onto the nonhuman world, but his beliefs do not lose touch with reality unless he becomes psychotic. The therapist does not usually become apathetic in listening to the concrete thinking of the psychotic patient because the delusions promote anxiety. It is the pseudorealis-tic, concrete thinking of the schizoid patient that is largely responsible for the therapist's apathetic response.

A moderately agoraphobic, female schizoid patient dwelled repetitively during each entire session on the state of her apartment. The therapist believed that the leaking, run-down apartment was a metaphor signifying the patient's frag-mented self. However, when the therapist interpreted that the apartment stood for the patient's self state, the patient insisted that she could distinguish the apartment from herself. The patient continued to show no capacity to symbolize and be-lieved that the therapist was accusing her of being crazy. She rejected his suggestions to have it repaired. The therapist was frustrated and then became apathetic.

There was a turning point when the therapist recognized that the motive for her suggestions was to stop the patient's complaining. Through this understanding, the therapist rec-ognized that the client needed the therapist to become in-tensely concerned and interested in the state of the apartment. The therapist joined the client in expressing interest in the apartment as if it were as precious as a human being or an infant. The therapist's response helped the patient to recog-nize that the apartment signified a human self state. Thus, during one session, as the patient and therapist animatedly discussed the apartment, the patient laughed and said that they were talking about it as if it were a person. The patient then saw that the apartment symbolized her own beleaguered sense of self. By joining the patient in treating the apartment as a human object, the therapist helped the patient begin to achieve metaphorical thinking.

Searles (1962) states that it is the awareness of emotion— whether murderousness, grief, affection, awareness of the

entire spectrum of emotion—that is the parent to metaphor
ical thought.

The patient may also manifest concrete thinking by dis
playing an attachment to the nonhuman aspects of the thera
peutic environment. Thus, one patient never expressed any
interest in the therapist as a person but was quite interested in
the paintings on the wall, the view from the window, the
furniture, and the rug. He eventually noticed the plants and
said he experienced comfort in the sessions by looking at the
plants. Eventually, he expressed separation anxiety at the end
of the session at having to leave the comforting room. At
intervals between sessions, he soothed himself by thinking of
the building, the elevator, the waiting room, the magazines
stacked on the table, and finally the therapeutic office. It was
only after a prolonged period of treatment that he told the
therapist that he could help him by sitting as still as the plants.
It was necessary that the therapist tolerate being related to as a
nonhuman object so that the patient could gradually allow
him to become alive and human. This recognition by the
patient also coincided with him becoming more alive and
human. He expressed a beginning recognition of the significance of the inanimate object world, saying, "I have always
been a collector of furniture, especially antiques. One could
love furniture and beautiful things for their own sake and
guess I do. But I suspect there is another motive operating.
Take a chair. When I get up from it and walk away I know it
isn't going anywhere. At least not by itself. It will be there
when I return. With people, you never know."

JEALOUSY OF AN INTERNAL OBJECT IN THE
TREATMENT OF THE SCHIZOID PATIENT

Searles (1986) has described how jealousy related to an internal object within the patient is a central factor in severe and

pervasive psychopathology and is responsible for a considerable amount of the unconscious resistance, on the parts of the
patient and analyst, to the analytic process. Such jealousy
phenomena are based upon powerful ego-splitting processes
derived from the early infant–mother relationship.

An adult female patient had difficulty concentrating upon
and completing professional tasks. Although she was bright
and creative, she would become distracted by other interests,
activities, projects, and so on. Whatever she undertook, she felt
that there was something else that she should be doing. An
inner critical voice also interfered by thinking that her efforts
were not adequate or worthy of completion. The critical voice
of the distracting thoughts of this patient as the expression of
an internal split-off object that was jealous of the patient's self-
interest. She remembered that during her adolescence, her
mother had always interrupted her when she practiced at the
piano, read, or was otherwise occupied. This jealousy of the
internal object derived from the early child–mother relationship in which the child was jealous of the mother's self-
involved activities that left out the child and the mother was
jealous of the child's self-involved activities that left out the
mother. In the treatment of the schizoid patient jealousy of the
internal object frequently becomes an important factor in the
transference–countertransference situation (Searles 1986).
The patient uses projective identification to place onto the
therapist a jealous self or object component to which the therapist responds by counter-identification (Grotstein 1985),
thereby assuming the position of the jealous object.

For instance, shortly after beginning treatment, an adult
female patient read a self-help book. Throughout her sessions,
she discussed the ideas of the book and its recommendations
for self-improvement, asking the therapist to clarify the
meaning of obscure passages. The therapist felt that she had
no other use for him except to serve as a translator of the book,
which she valued more than the therapist. The therapist felt

jealous over her relationship to the book, became overtly critical of it, and interpreted her use of it as a resistance to treatment. The patient replied that the therapist was competitive with the author and wanted her to be dependent only upon him. In this situation, the transference–countertransference situation recapitulated the early child–mother relationship in which the parent was jealous and intruded upon the child's efforts to separate and individuate.

A male adult patient spoke in his sessions as if he were talking to himself or to the furniture in the room, never pausing so that the therapist could respond, and not seeming to care if the therapist understood what he was saying. On the few occasions when the therapist commented, the patient ignored the therapist's remarks and continued his monologue as if the therapist had never spoken. The therapist felt left out of the patient's relationship with himself; the therapist felt he was of no use or value to the patient. Increasingly, the therapist interrupted the patient's monologues with questions or comments that the patient found annoying. The therapist became jealous at being left out of the patient's exclusive relationship with himself and felt the need to be noticed by the patient. During these sessions, the therapist felt disturbingly as if he was invisible or did not exist for the patient in the same way that the patient had felt invisible in the presence of his extremely narcissistic primary caregiver.

HATE IN THE COUNTERTRANSFERENCE

The patient's lack of significant emotional dependence upon the therapist is a defense against the emergence of relating to the therapist as a subjective object. Winnicott (1947) describes how the schizoid patient's need for the object is ruthless in its urgency, similar to the infant's need to achieve satisfaction without concern for the object. The schizoid patient may therefore treat the therapist and other significant objects as if they were slaves, existing only to respond to the patient's need for instinctual gratification and ego care, and to be discarded once the patient is satisfied. Winnicott (1956) states that these patients may also act out through antisocial behavior, which is fundamentally a sign of hope in that the patient protests against early deprivations. The apathy that pervades the therapeutic relationship is fundamentally a defense against the emergence of extreme and ruthless dependence on the subjective object in the transference. As Winnicott (1947) points out, the patient's ruthless needs in the transference typically induce hatred in the countertransference. If the therapist is uncomfortable in accepting hate in the countertransference, he may use intellectual understanding of the patient's early deprivations and pseudoempathy as a defense against his own hating responses.

A male patient began his treatment with a female therapist describing the various ways he exploited and abused other females, stole from other persons, even his friends, and faced possible jail time. He stated that if he were locked up, he would kill himself.

As the therapist listened, she felt frightened and wondered if he would harm her in some way since he had even harmed his friends. She continually had the thought, "He would sell his own mother for an easy dollar." She had the uncomfortable thought that he deserved to be locked up and that she did not care if he killed himself, that it might be better for the community and everyone concerned if he were to do so. She was extremely uncomfortable about her negative feelings, and wondered if she had the capacity to work with him. In subsequent sessions, whenever she felt fearful or angry, she forced herself to remember that he had been a victimized and deprived child. She did not confront the de-

structiveness of his antisocial acting out, but rather remarked
upon how he must have felt powerless, deprived, or helpless
when he described ripping off or victimizing others. He
responded by self-righteously proclaiming that he had a right
to steal books and clothes since they were overpriced or that a
person whom he ripped off was as much a thief, in his own
way, as the patient, and therefore deserved to be robbed. He
acted quite seductively toward the therapist and then sometimes said that he could not afford to pay for a session, or
arrived late but demanded that she see him over the scheduled
time or called her all hours of the night and became enraged if
she was not available to speak with him. Increasingly, he
manipulated and exploited her, and she felt as if she were
losing her professional role with him. In fact, she became
aware that when she interpreted how he felt vulnerable, helpless or frightened, it was actually she herself who felt these
disturbing feelings in response to him.

Winnicott (1947) states that the analysis of the severely
disturbed patient becomes impossible unless the analyst's
own hate is conscious and sorted out. He says that no matter
how much the therapist understands and empathizes with the
severely disturbed patient, he cannot avoid fearing and hating
him at times. The therapist must sort out and study his *objective*
responses to patients, including his hate, especially in the
treatment of schizoid and antisocial patients. The therapist can
come to a sincere, empathic caring for the schizoid patient but
this will occur only after he has sorted out his responses of fear
and hatred and helped the patient work through his ruthless,
antisocial behavioral patterns. The therapist's intellectual empathic understanding of the patient's early deprivations, the
basic fault, and so forth, is important and should be remembered but not used as a defense because of the therapist's guilt
in response to objective fear and hate in the countertransference. In the case of the therapist described above, her initial
fear and guilt were a signal that this patient, who she felt

could sell his mother for a dollar, might well attempt to treat her in a similar fashion. Thus, the objective countertransference was adaptive and self-preservative.

Winnicott, in his article on "Hate in the Counter-Transference" (1947) described his treatment of a 9-year-old boy with anti-social symptoms. The boy had been placed in a hostel for evacuated children during World War II and was in need of treatment for his habitual truancy. However, he ran away as he had been doing since the age of 6. He turned up in a police station very near Winnicott's home, and Winnicott's wife generously took him in for three months that Winnicott described as three months of hell. During the first phase of his treatment, he was given complete freedom and spending money whenever he wished. When he turned up at a police station, he had only to telephone and Winnicott fetched him at once. Interpretations were made at all hours, day or night, as the situation required.

Winnicott states that he never hit the youngster, despite his frustration, thanks to his awareness of his objective countertransferential hate. However, in crisis he would physically take the youngster, without anger or blame, and leave him outside the house, whatever the weather or the hour of the day. There was a special bell the boy could ring for readmittance as soon as he recovered from his maniacal attack. Each time, as Winnicott put the boy outside, he told him that what had happened made him hate the boy. Saying this enabled Winnicott to tolerate the situation without losing his temper, letting go, or murdering him.

Winnicott states that the mother typically hates the baby before the baby hates the mother; in fact before the baby knows the mother hates him, that the mother hates the baby from the beginning. In his view, the mother hates the infant because the baby is not her own mental conception; it is not magically produced, it is a danger to her body in pregnancy and during birth; it interferes with her private life, her freedom; it hurts her nipples or tries to hurt her; it is ruthless, treats her as scum, a slave. Having got what he wants, he discards her; he refuses her food, makes her doubt her capacity as a good mother but may smile at a stranger and eat for another; and he knows nothing of all that she does, of how much she sacrifices for him.

Winnicott states that in the intensive treatment of the severely disturbed patient, the therapist finds himself in a position comparable to that of the mother of the newborn infant. The patient will not be able to tolerate his hatred of the therapist unless the therapist can hate him. It is through the acceptance of hatred in the transference–countertransference situation that the love associated with therapeutic regression can emerge.

LOVE IN THE COUNTERTRANSFERENCE

The patient internalizes the therapist as a loving object. There are two reactions. On the one hand, the patient experiences the therapist as a good object providing ego care and fostering growth. At the same time, the therapist is experienced as an exciting object. The excitement generates anxiety because the patient experiences the allure of symbiosis. It must be remembered that the schizoid patient feels an inner deadness or emptiness. As he becomes excited in response to the therapist's efforts to reach him, he begins to feel libidinally alive. The patient feels the excitement a baby feels as it discovers it is loved by the mother. The patient will not be helped unless the therapist can reach his infantile self in this way. The patient will at first be frightened and endeavor to reject the therapist's help.

Joan was a severely deprived 7-year-old youngster. In session, she sat stiffly, neither playing nor making contact with the therapist. There was a bottle of soap bubbles on the play table that she looked at with interest. Once, she said she was sick but would not elaborate upon the nature of her illness. Pointing to the soap bubbles, she said "medicine." In the next session, she again said "sick" and later indicated that I should give her the medicine. I played at feeding her the medicine with a spoon and she knocked my hand away. I tried again and she continued to knock my hand away. I did not try to force her to take the medicine, nor did I give up. I directed the spoon toward her mouth in what became a rhythmic gesture and she knocked it away rhythmically. Before long, the giving of the medicine and the knocking it away became a rhythmic dance between me and the patient. It became clear that we were beginning to relate to each other through the rhythmic play. She suddenly pretended to take the medicine.

Later, the girl described how she had been rejected by her mother, who also taught her that she should not trust anyone in the world. The girl rejected me in the way she had been rejected by the mother. She is also loyal to her mother in rejecting a world her mother told her was untrustworthy. In order to help her, I had to become impervious to the rejection. The medicine was the equivalent of love. She was unsure if it was good, healing love, or poison.

There is an overriding principle operating in the holding relationship. Unconsciously, the patient finds in the therapist the protective mothering figure and the patient feels loved as a person in his own right. Guntrip (1969) wrote of the therapeutic value of love in the countertransference. I understand love to mean that the therapist reaches the inner self of the patient, causing him to feel cared for and valued in his own right.

There are manifold ways that the patient may need the therapist to serve as a holding object. There may be a need for the therapist to be available by telephone and for extra appointments. The patient expresses the full range of his anxiety, panic, depression, and destructiveness for the therapist to contain. The therapist's task is to survive and help the patient to survive (Winnicott 1954). The patient must find the therapist to be a good enough object in reality to risk releasing his bad objects (Fairbairn 1943). The release of inner bad object is of great value to the patient. He may release the bad objects directly into the transference (Seinfeld 1990) or may ventilate about past, present, and anticipated life problems.

DIRECT INTERPRETATIONS

Schizoid patients are often deficient in positive introjects and dominated by negative introjects. The holding relationship aims toward building positive introjects. Direct interpretations attempt to dissolve negative introjects. The therapist provides a protective relationship to the vulnerable infantile self, but confronts the destructiveness of the patient's sadistic persecution of the infantile self. The patient may then direct his rage toward the therapist instead of the infantile self. Once the self-abuse ceases, the therapist may empathize with the patient's efforts to gain strength by identifying with the abusive, powerful object. It must be remembered that the infantile self is libidinally connected and loyal to the internal persecutor. The forceful interpretations by the therapist actually permit the internal persecutor to relax its hold on the vulnerable self, since there is the sense that the therapist will have the strength to help the patient. The inner persecution is an effort to keep a weak ego going in the only way the patient knows. There is a fear of letting the bad object go because there may be no object at all. This anxiety is sometimes manifested in the patient's playful observation that if he did not have his complaints, there would be nothing to discuss in therapy.

Beyond the tie to the bad object, the patient has extinguished his need for the good object that was felt as empty. In giving up the bad object, the patient fears that there will be nothing to say, that he will encounter his inner emptiness, that he will have no desire. Guntrip's withdrawn, passive, regressed ego (1969) is actually an infantile self that has renounced needs in order to be accepted by the object. This emptiness is felt as dull and flat. The patient and therapist ultimately dread arriving at the point of nothingness—the empty core. This is characterized by both patient and therapist feeling that there is no place to begin and nothing to say. The therapist must allow for the experience of deadness in the transference–countertransference. Eventually, the therapist directly interprets that the patient has remained emotionally dead to be accepted by the object. If the patient and therapist have not experienced this nothingness in the therapeutic encounter, the direct interpretation is experienced only intellectually.

The schizoid patient experiences the extinction of all needs as a symbiotic bond with the rejecting object. Thus, the patient longs for and dreads the bond of emotional deadness. In the transference–countertransference situation, the patient and therapist reach the point of emptiness, nothingness, nihilism. The patient needs nothing of value from the therapist and feels loved for being an infant without needs. The therapist tolerates the patient not needing him and making him useless but also interprets this state as ceasing to need in order to please the object. The therapist might then explain how need-satisfying behavior toward nonhuman objects replaced the desire for love. The child is given candy rather than maternal attention. The giving of things is a compensation and replaces the giving of love. The dead silence between patient and therapist increasingly becomes a therapeutic regression.

Once the patient ceases to replace the need for love with the compulsive need for things, and when he allows himself to encounter the extinguishing of the need for love, he begins to direct desire toward the human object world. In sessions, he sees that there is no place to begin and nothing to discuss except where he himself chooses to begin and what he himself chooses to discuss. In this way, the encounter with nothingness leads to autonomy and creativity. The encounter with the basic fault is initially the experience of a static emptiness sometimes personified by a baby without needs. In not filling the empty core with things and in understanding its earlier feeling state, the empty core has the opportunity to become dynamic, and the experience of the desire for love becomes a possibility. The patient feels cared about for being alive. This feeling gives rise to the genuine interests and desires of the true self.

SCHIZOID ISSUES IN THE COUNTERTRANSFERENCE

There has been much exploration within psychoanalysis as to when the therapist goes beyond the classical boundaries based upon his own emotional needs and not the patient's. The focus on countertransference relates to the depressive position and the analyst's need to deny aggression and rescue his own injured object. It may also be based on oedipal issues of forbidden gratification.

In the history of psychoanalysis, the oedipal and depressive positions were discovered before the developmentally earlier schizoid position. The discovery of the schizoid position suggests that therapists may also emotionally withhold, not because of the patient's needs, but because of their own needs. Therapists may not only suffer from guilt and urges to rescue clients, but from inner emptiness and an inability to provide for patients. It is time to look more closely at the countertransference reaction, in which the therapist chronically feels that difficult patients are sucking him dry, are overly dependent, are manipulative and in need of constant limits and boundaries. My contention is not that severe patients always become greedy, overly dependent, and so forth. I raise the question of how frequently these therapists' sense of emptiness can make severely disturbed patients seem impossible to treat.

The countertransferential schizoid reaction may have influenced psychoanalysis from the start. The classical technique, with its emphasis on emotional distance has been related to schizoid anxieties. Freud placed patients on the couch and sat behind them partially because of his discomfort of being looked at by patients. Fairbairn was among the first analysts to demonstrate that schizoid patients need a holding relationship. Schoenewolf (1990b) believes that Fairbairn's actual technique was too neutral and distant, especially given his theoretical views. I believe that Fairbairn suffered from countertransferential schizoid reactions.

EMPATHIZING WITH THE PATIENT'S PARANOIDLIKE UNDERSTANDING RELATED TO THE ENGULFING OBJECT

In conclusion, the therapist needs to be especially sensitive to the patient's anxieties about engulfment. For example, the therapist working with a schizoid who finds it difficult to meet the demands of society in terms of surrendering freedom should empathically acknowledge this issue. Gradually, the therapist helps the patient to think about whether decisions are for self or for others. The therapist helps the patient think about choices in a nonengulfing way. The therapist provides or refrains from mirroring, depending upon the patient's need.

10

THE LONG-TERM TREATMENT OF THE SCHIZOID PATIENT

The schizoid individual meets the demands of life by compulsively driven activity that protects a regressed and fragile self. These patients suffer from ego weakness and have been deprived of the supportive parenting environment that would have prepared them for the demands of work and relationships. They outwardly drive themselves to function but inwardly long to run away from coping with daily existence. They develop a weak foundation for later personality development. They have not felt loved in their own right.

The autonomous self of the infant is in need of a supportive object relationship in which to live, to thrive, and to grow. When basic object-relational needs go unmet, the self remains weak, helpless, and overridden by instinctual urges, which become desperate in an effort to compensate for the failure to be loved. In finding oneself alone, the child cannot shoulder the ordinary demands of life. He suffers from the basic fault (Balint 1968), a deficiency at the foundation of psychic structure that threatens the collapse of the ego. The last resort is to drive oneself intensely forward and to whip oneself into line. The severity over oneself provides a sense of power and wards off feelings of helplessness. In this self-hate, the individual identifies with the parental figure who rejected his longing for love. When there is no way out for the infantile self that is persecuted, the person may want to die to escape the inner persecution and the burdens of living. There is the wish for peace and a retreat.

In the treatment of the schizoid, the primary task of the therapist is to reach the frightened, regressed self (Guntrip 1969) and provide it with the holding, supportive relationship essential for ego growth. The therapist enters the inner world of the patient, where support may neutralize the assaults of the persecutory object. My approach to therapy includes emotional holding and direct interpretation of unconscious object-relational conflicts. In the treatment of schizoid patients, I endeavor to find a way into the patient's inner world, where I can be used as an anchor in order to find a path to the outer world. In this process the patient does not usually lose the therapist internally. If the therapist can reach the inner self of the schizoid patient, there is hope for emotional rebirth and object-related individuation. The following long-term case report describes this process.

THE CASE OF ESTELLE

Estelle, a middle-aged single woman, attractive and casual in dress, was employed as a librarian. Initially she sought treatment because throughout much of her life she had been serving others as a transitional object. She had grown resentful from extending herself to others and getting little back. Currently in analytic treatment three times weekly for nearly six years, she started out once weekly and gradually increased the frequency of sessions.

Personal History

Estelle grew up in an intact family with a gruff, domineering mother and an absentminded, laid-back father who had been a college professor until he suffered a debilitating stroke in Estelle's early adolescence.

Estelle recalled much of her childhood in the context of vicious fights between her mother and her older sister. Her mother was described as short and squat with a strikingly ugly face. The sister, a rebellious, attractive adolescent, joined local streetwise peer groups, dressed and groomed like them, and was frequently in trouble for drinking bouts, truancy, and escapades with boys. The mother made it a point of personal honor not to allow the sister to have her own way. The two became locked in a cruel struggle.

Estelle was the compliant child and attributed her passivity to witnessing the battering of her sister, especially after the sister was permanently banished from the home.

Estelle's life as a transitional object grew out of the relationship with her mother. She orbited around the mother's wishes and served as an admirer, confidante, and companion. The mother was a self-preoccupied woman who could talk incessantly, often exhausting the hapless listener, and not be aware of it. On her own, the mother enjoyed traveling, attended social functions, and contributed to the community. She was genuinely supportive of Estelle's efforts to succeed, providing her with financial assistance for college and later helping with living expenses.

Estelle came to the Northeast to attend college and upon graduation remained, finding full-time employment as a librarian. She enjoyed music, literature, and writing but conversed in a concrete, flat, obsessional manner. The therapist was surprised years later when Estelle evidenced a flair for language and writing. She was the quintessential example of the split between a concrete, colorless, and superficial conscious waking life, and a complex, poetic, unconscious fantasy life.

Being for Others

The patient came for treatment because she repeatedly allowed herself to be taken advantage of by friends, family and professional colleagues. Her generosity towards others was rarely reciprocated. Estelle chauffeured her close friend to medical and therapy appointments, spent the night at Betty's house because Betty was lonely, and so on. If the situation was reversed Betty would hardly extend herself. Betty was representative of others Estelle helped but then felt taken advantage by. The therapist gradually had the impression that Estelle devoted herself to needy, infantile, borderline patients who then distanced themselves because of their merger anxieties. Estelle felt betrayed and rejected. She would become depressed and could not concentrate fully at work, would go in late, and begin to neglect herself.

Estelle had, on occasion, some sexual contact with women friends, but she did not identify herself as homosexual. She said she enjoyed the warmth of physical holding but was uncomfortable about stimulation of erotogenic zones. She never had sexual intercourse with a man but she did have sexual contacts that were pleasurable but generated anxiety. She stated that her close, personal relationships were with women, and she felt more of an emotional hunger for their love and acceptance, though on a purely physical level she preferred men. She did not feel like a sexual person and generally preferred holding and companionship to sex of any kind.

The Analysis of the Bad Object in the Schizoid Condition

In the first two years of treatment, the therapist intervened by focusing on the patient's longing for symbiosis and the tie to the bad object. This is a focus that I described at great length in a previous work (Seinfeld 1990). I shall remark upon it briefly as it pertains to the schizoid condition. The patient primarily complained that she put herself out selflessly for her friend Betty and the latter did not appreciate her sufficiently. She was jealous of Betty's other relationships or activities separate from Estelle. It was apparent that underlying these complaints was pervasive separation anxiety. I initially intervened by identifying the symbiotic quality of their relationship and the underlying separation anxiety. It was not difficult to compare the domineering, demanding, and infantile characteristics of the actual mother and the comparable personality traits of the current mother substitutes. Thus, Estelle was quickly made to see that current objects of her life such as Betty represented the internal mother image and this insight afforded her initial relief.

There was one important feature of this substitute symbiotic relationship that characterized it as schizoid (on Estelle's part) and dictated a technique that differed from similar interventions with borderline patients. In her relationship with Betty and other maternal substitutes, Estelle was always on the giving side. In actuality, she rarely asked her friends for any comfort, love, or help, but rather provided nurturance on the condition that the other person would not abandon her. The typical borderline patient is more than likely to be on the taking side of a dependent relationship. These patients disassociate their own infantile, emotionally hungry selves by projective identification into the partner of the symbioticlike union. Thus Betty represented not only the maternal image but also Estelle's disassociated, infantile, needy self. Betty served as a fitting container for the maternal and infantile self-images in that she was herself, in reality, demanding, domineering, and infantile. So long as Betty remained dependent upon Estelle, the latter did not experience her own infantile dependence or separation anxiety. It was only when Betty began to create distance with aggression that Estelle became frightened and sought help. This relationship was a reliving of her relationship to her mother in that she and the mother had unconsciously exchanged roles and she often had served in the parental role to an infantile, dependent mother.

Implications for Therapeutic Technique

In the treatment of similar schizoid patients, I initially interpret their tie to the other in terms of the bond to the maternal image, but I do not interpret the projection of the infantile, needy self into the other. This disassociation is often necessary for the patient to remain object-related. In other words, if Estelle were to own and experience the infantile hungry self before her ego was sufficiently strengthened in ongoing treatment, it would be opening up a bottomless pit and prematurely exposing her ego weakness. She would then have no alternative but to either lose herself in the insatiable hunger for objects or completely withdraw from object relations. These patients can only relate to the object world in the role of helper. Therefore, it is a major blunder to attempt to aid the patient in becoming more assertive and to stop others entirely from taking advantage of them. In those instances in which the therapist illustrates to the patient the endless ways that people take advantage of him and provides him with a crash course in self-assertion, the schizoid patient will feel humiliated and lost. The patient may have no other way of relating except through the parentified helping mode. In addition, the patient is made to feel both a fool and weak for a mode of relating that may be the only source of self-esteem. Therapists sometimes confuse the schizoid disorder with the much higher level masochistic neurosis. In the latter disorder, the patient also tends to sacrifice himself for others and suffer as a result, but this behavior is determined primarily by unconscious guilt and the fear of aggression. The masochistic personality is capable of relating to others through other than masochistic modes if this defense is modified. The schizoid patient does not have this option available.

In work with schizoid patients, I enlist their active ego functioning in determining where to draw the line in sacrificing themselves. I might state, "You have the capacity to give of yourself to others and to care for others, which certainly helps your relationships. It is good both for you and for the other. The difficulty is that sometimes your sacrifice seems

to take too much out of you and this hurts both the relationship and yourself. I want to be as clear as I can: the issue is not
that you give of yourself—rather, it's that we need to think
when it is at too great a cost to yourself."

At one time, I had said to patients that the distinguishing
line occurred when the patient helped another at his own
expense. However, a patient corrected me, stating "It is often
at my expense. If I help someone who is incapable and do
something for them and get nothing directly back it *is* at my
expense—that is not the place to draw the line. The question is
when the cost is too much at my expense."

The treatment aim is to get the patient himself to think of
when the cost is too high. Individuated functioning is en-
hanced but to a manageable degree. When Estelle and I explored this issue, she suddenly became anxious, realizing the
full implications. She said, "I'm beginning to see. There is a
point where I've gone too far, where I've given of myself to
the point where I'm emptied. But that point is something I
must find for myself. Neither you nor anyone else can tell me.
It may be different today than it is tomorrow. There is no point
at which giving is too much except when it is too much for me,
where I find it to be too much. So I create the point."

There is another essential issue that the therapist needs to
be aware of. Sometimes after Estelle and I would discuss such
issues, she would put herself out for a friend and claim that it
was manageable and of her own choice. In the days to follow,
she would feel increasingly depleted, apathetic, and sometimes
suicidal. She would make no connection between the self-
sacrifice and her sense of existential futility. It seemed that her
despair came out of the blue and she wondered if it were not
biologically based. I would then tell her that her despair is
signalling that she has gone over the line, where self-sacrifice
becomes too costly. In actuality, it took a long time for me to
become aware of this connection; it was a gradual process, but
once she was able to listen to her despair as a signal she was
better able to regulate her giving in relationships.

The idea that giving of oneself can provide its own
emotional rewards and is a natural response to feeling filled

and cared for is a basic principle of the Fairbairn object relational viewpoint. It is only from the standpoint of pathological narcissism that giving will always be viewed as masochistic. Thus, the therapist endeavors to help the patient arrive at a more mature basis for nurturing. Taking precedes over giving in developmental chronology. The individual must be given and take in enough love, he must know how to take care of himself, how to say no when necessary, to be secure, and to enjoy his own intake. As a result, there is a natural inclination to give or to give back. Estelle's giving was not resting on a foundation of taking or on a secure self. It was only later that Estelle felt emotionally rewarded by caring for a friend and seeing the friend genuinely enjoy herself. The therapist affirmed the positive value of Estelle's caring for other persons in themselves.

The Paradox: Being for the Other Becomes a Mode of Being for Oneself

The therapist helps the schizoid patient by helping the individual to think independently about where to draw the line in being-for-others. The therapeutic paradox is that in allowing the patient to be for others as much or as little as one determines for oneself, the therapist creates a situation in which being-for-others becomes the patient's own autonomous mode of being and therefore also a mode of being. It may be that the patient's caregiver wanted her only to be for the parent and not for anyone else. She may have rebelled from the parents' hold on her by transferring this mode of being for others onto persons other than her mother. Thus the germ of individuation may be situated in the realm of being-for-others. The therapist who endeavors to direct the patient to a new mode of being may thereby be inadvertently assuming the role of the caregiver, perceived to be jealous of the patient's interest in other persons. These subtleties must be actively kept in mind in the treatment of schizoid patients. In

Estelle's case, her mother did not interfere with her attempts at achievement in academic pursuits, hobbies, or interests that she pursued independently. The mother was threatened by Estelle's interests and friendships. Thus, Estelle's mode of being-for-others could also be understood as a means of individuation.

Schizoid Despair

After four years of therapy she functioned autonomously with greater ease, was less destructively dependent upon friends and less persecuted by the internal bad object. She was aware that formerly she had gone through life as an automaton, doing whatever was expected. She now reported feeling less on automatic pilot, better able to discern what activities were depleting and taking more interest in her life. Therefore, I was surprised by the following event. The patient returned from a short visit to her mother's home during which she impulsively took one of her mother's hypodermic syringes. The mother was a nurse. This act had a dissociated quality. She experienced the impulse as overwhelming, a necessity. There was a vague sense of needing the syringe in the event that she decided to kill herself. She could think of nothing in the visit itself that seemed eventful, that could account for her overwhelming depression. It felt as if she had just plunged into a pit of despair. In the ensuing weeks, Estelle described a growing sense of apathy and despondency, culminating in an active obsession with suicide.

Schizoid Isolation

It is important to distinguish the sense of schizoid isolation that Estelle experienced from the abandonment depression suffered by the borderline patient. The latter, experiencing separation/individuation in the course of treatment, fears losing the good object and the symbiotic union. In anticipatio of the dreaded object loss, the borderline patient become depressed. There is a reliving of the withdrawal of the objec associated with the patient's earlier endeavors at separatio (Masterson 1976). The abandonment depression of the bor derline may be understood as a mild schizoid state in compar ison to the schizoid patient's terror of losing all objects, in ternal and external.

In advancing Fairbairn's theory, Guntrip (1969) con tended that the ultimate dread of the schizoid patient is the los of all objects, the terror of an objectless state. Estelle fel isolated, apathetic, with no desire to live and nothing to liv for. She could make no sense of what accounted for her plung into this hopeless despair. She felt like withdrawing; she took no pleasure in life. Fairbairn (1943) believed that the patien remained libidinally tied to the internal bad object because i was better than no (outer) object all. Guntrip (1969) added tha it was even worse to have no internal object at all.

Estelle's plunge into despair began during the visit to he mother. She was gradually separating from the internal perse cutory object. This led me to think that thoughts of suicid with mother's weapon (syringe) had to do with the retaliatior of her mother as well as the wish to finally separate from mother by killing her image off with her own weapon. De pression related to the bad object is characterized by self persecution, helplessness, self-hate, and the inclination toward restitution. Depression related to an objectless, schizoid state is marked by hopelessness, apathy, futility, lack of purpose and of meaning.

Schizoid patients feel such despair with violent sudden ness. The therapist must be active and direct in interventions. Suicidal urges in any patient is of concern but the schizoid patient is often in greater danger than the borderline because of the tendency to withdraw from potentially helpful object relations and because of the rapidity of the plunge into despair. The schizoid becomes hopeless and withdrawn, unlike the borderline who becomes helpless and needy.

nternalization of the Therapist as Object-Insurance

Given the schizoid patient's potential to quickly enter into states of objectless futility, I work directly toward becoming internalized from the beginning of treatment to insure that later, when the patient is faced with the threat of an objectless state, I can draw upon the internal therapeutic relationship to keep the patient connected. In the case of Estelle, I tracked her remembrance of the therapeutic relationship, or lack thereof, in intervals between sessions, impressing upon her the importance of internally maintaining our relationship so that she did not have to be alone in her psyche and therefore overburdened with life. Schizoid patients are well known for being hypersensitive to ordinary environmental setbacks, impingements, disappointments, and the like (Meissner 1988). This extreme sensitivity is based upon being alone internally with only negative introjects. The schizoid patient's defenses against the internalization of a good object are so great that the therapist will not be internalized over time naturally through empathizing and listening. If the therapist does not take active steps toward this internalization, the patient may go through the motions of treatment for a prolonged period but experience little personality change.

From the beginning of my treatment of Estelle, I asked how she experienced our relationship between sessions and encouraged her to try to maintain a remembrance of it. After initially broaching the subject with the patient, I ask for associations. Estelle stated that my remarks made sense but she was uncertain how to accomplish holding onto a positive image of the relationship. In the very next session, she spoke of overhearing women speak of a sensuous therapist who had sex with his patients. When the therapist actively endeavors to become internalized as a good object, the schizoid patient will typically consciously react as if the therapist is pursuing an appropriate function as a good object, but unconsciously the patient will experience the intervention as a seduction by the libidinally exciting object. Estelle provided clear evidence of

fearing the therapist as an exciting object by alluding to th
sensuous therapist. Other patients may be less verbal in thei
reaction. For instance, another patient, Diane, did not respond
verbally but would miss sessions or not call me as planned t
touch base during depressive suicidal periods. In these situations, I immediately interpret the patient's negative reaction t
the therapist's endeavor to become internalized as a goo
object.

I pointed out to Estelle how in the previous session I had
remarked upon the importance of internalizing our relationship, and that immediately afterward she spoke of women she
had overheard discussing a sensuous therapist. I asked if there
could be a connection. She became embarrassed, denied being
aware of any. I stated that it was possible that she unconsciously feared my remarks as a seduction, that there may have
been a question as to whether I was a sensual therapist. I said
there were understandable reasons why she might have this
concern. First, one hears of situations in which therapists act
unprofessionally or unethically and seduce patients. Estelle
said that when she had heard the women discussing the sensuous therapist she thought of other incidents she had heard
of. Then she admitted to wondering fleetingly about me as
well but dismissed the possibility. She reminded herself of
what I had said about the internalization of the therapy in a
very professional manner, explained my reasons on her personal history, problems, and the objectives of our work. I
stated that she may have reassured herself but a residue of
doubt probably remained, understandably, since she did not
know me very well yet. After she acknowledged this and I
assured her of my position, I also stated that a patient's own
wishes could also be a contributing factor in wondering if the
therapist might be a sensuous therapist.

When the therapist endeavors to become internalized as a
good object or makes himself available to the patient during
crises or periods of emotional upset by, for example, permitting phone calls, or providing extra appointments, the
schizoid patient does experience this loosening of the thera-

peutic frame as both a seduction by the exciting object and a serious effort by the therapist to help. The therapist must always be aware of both levels of response and be prepared to bring the subject up for direct discussion. The therapist should provide strong emotional support and become internalized as a good object but also directly interpret the patient's preconscious and unconscious negative reactions. Patients will have their reactions regardless of the sex of patient and therapist.

I was available to Estelle during this difficult time, offering extra phone contacts and appointments. When she came in telling me how depressed and hopeless she may have been the day before, I asked what had happened to our relationship in that she felt all alone. When she told me how hopeless she felt for the future, I asked why she had forgotten I would be there to help her through it. In addition, I interpreted that as she gave up the bad aspects of her tie to her mother, she feared she would have nothing left inside. Estelle weathered this first emotional storm but there remained her sense of not knowing what to expect from life.

The Inability to Desire

The analysis of Estelle's continued apathy brought forth the issue that as she separated from others, she had no idea how to discover her own needs. Winnicott refers to this point as the analysis of the false self (1960). Now that Estelle was separating more from objects, she had no idea what she desired. I said, "You have no experience in wanting things for yourself, only in knowing what others want you to want."

She recalled memories that demonstrated the dominance of false self-relatedness. Her mother insisted that the family visit with relatives. Estelle wished to remain near home with her adolescent friends. The mother replied that Estelle would be crazy to remain at home when she could be visiting her favorite cousins, enjoying her favorite food, and so on. How could she even think of staying home with her do-nothing friends? The mother had her own anxieties about seeing these relatives, did not like them, but felt that she had to visit. She actually wanted Estelle present for moral support. Estelle now saw that the mother denied her own dependence and invented reasons for Estelle's joining her.

As Estelle separated emotionally from objects, she realized that often what she had thought she wanted was what another person wished her to want. I did not direct her to want anything but made it clear that I wanted her to become a person who could know and choose for herself. This is a difficult technique in work with the schizoid patient. The patient often feels lost at not knowing what to want. If the patient looks to the therapist for answers, and the therapist does not respond but instead redirects the question to, "What it is that *you* want?" the patient will feel abandoned—that the therapist does not care. Therefore, when I do not take over this function for the patient, I explain why in terms of the person-to-person relationship to the patient. With Estelle, I said, "I am not telling you what to want, because I wish for you to become a person who can desire for yourself and choose for yourself." I remind these patients that the problem is that others directed them toward what they should want, and it would not help if I did the same. Given the serious threat of object loss in these patients, I initially include myself in the wording of the intervention by saying, "I want you to become a person who can desire for yourself." The patient dreads desiring for himself because it is experienced as an abandonment. Therefore, the patient often needs to feel that there is a transitional object that wants him to want something for himself. In this way, he internalizes the idea of the object wanting him to want for himself and does not feel utterly alone.

The Emergence of the Autonomous Self

Estelle was a hard-working, responsible, competent person. Her job at the university did not demand that she be creative or emotionally involved. It required attention to details and categorization, at which she excelled. Estelle typically depended upon others to create interest and direction while she energetically executed their plans. For instance, Betty and other friends usually knew what they wanted, but were too depressed and helpless to effect it. Thus Betty and Estelle complemented one another in their strengths and weaknesses.

The first sign of Estelle's autonomy emerged when she and her friends planned a party. Betty, the informal leader of the group, decided on the guest list, the food, the music, and the decor. Estelle discovered that she had her own preferences and did not want to depend only upon Betty's decisions and taste. She showed less dependence and the beginnings of oedipal rivalry (who had better taste?) with the mothering object. In the ensuing months, the autonomous self emerged in Estelle's pleasure in shopping, selection of clothes, and recreational activities. She expressed a preference for certain films she saw. Her descriptions of friends reflected opinions as to whom she liked and disliked. These changes were reflective of an awakening of her healthy narcissism. The therapeutic task in this period was primarily that of mirroring and providing Estelle with a reflection for the emergence of her true self.

At this time, we did not primarily discuss problems except how Estelle was never aware that she had always wanted what others chose for her. She was becoming successful professionally. She received a major promotion and a considerable raise in salary. It was especially impressive that she negotiated the job improvement, thinking through what responsibilities and functions she wanted. She was so successful that a major library in Europe invited her to visit, expenses paid, to consult.

Existential Futility

In the growth of the autonomous self, the schizoid patient may experience severe crisis. Major turning points may be marked by "existential futility." It might have been expected that Estelle would triumph and be successful in achieving her goals. However, once again she felt profound depression. She did not experience self-reproaches that might have reflected unconscious guilt over oedipal triumphs. Instead, she experienced a profound hopelessness and despair. She could feel neither joy nor enthusiasm about her new position. Everything was for naught. Her achievements were pointless. To the therapist's astonishment, she made out a will and spoke of tying up loose ends so that she could commit suicide.

Isolation

Estelle experienced the achievement of some of her goals as a threat to her object relations. On the surface it seemed that her life and relationships were improved considerably. In addition to her job promotion, she had made additional women friends and was also having both an emotional and sexual relationship with a man. She continued to complain about feeling more isolated and empty than ever before. Her significant objects were not moving away, yet she felt increasingly abandoned. She was the one withdrawing but felt that everyone was abandoning her. Interpretations pointing to this abandonment depression had no effect. She finally pointed the way to understanding her recent despair in saying that she considered herself as a stage in the lives of people who would inevitably outgrow her.

She had recently read an article that mentioned the transitional object, and she said this term fit her perfectly. She explored how she had served others as a transitional object throughout her life, beginning with her mother. We discussed how she was always on the giving end in relationships. We spent a session discussing her relationship with Betty and others. She felt better, but the sense of the meaninglessness of her existence returned. She felt confused. There was a growing uncertainty whether she would always be alone and she wondered if therapy could help. She wondered if she came to therapy for me, for herself, for her friends. Betty told her that therapy was helping her. Did she come to therapy for Betty or for herself? Maybe she should entirely break with Betty, her mother, and all symbiotic relationships. Sometimes she felt that Betty and I were somehow together against her. She did not want to come to therapy any longer for Betty or for me. She did not want to do anything for anyone but herself.

Being-for-Herself

Estelle said she was reviewing her gains in therapy. On paper it looked miraculous. A new job with a raise, new friendships, the first relationship with a man who shared her intellectual and cultural interests and sexual pleasure. She felt that the progress may not have been for herself but for the therapist. She said that it was true he never directed her in what to do. Nevertheless she could see that he was pleased with her improvement. The problem now was that she did not know if her accomplishments were for herself or to please him. She said, "I do not want to do anything for you any longer."

AN ANALYSIS OF THE TREATMENT

Earlier in the treatment, the patient needed to experience therapeutic mirroring to arrive at a beginning capacity to wish and to choose. The patient was accurate that she was not improving her functioning for herself but rather for the therapist. She would become more autonomous through finding herself mirrored in the therapist's response. It could be said that she was being independent for the therapist. For this reason, the therapist provided minimal direction. She now arrived at the stage at which she realized that she was captured in the reflection of the mirroring other. It is this realization that triggers differentiation. If the therapist had been overly involved in actively directing the patient's life, she may not have had the psychic space to recognize her dependent position.

The autonomous self now took a further step in growth—she decided she would act only for herself and not for the therapist, Betty, or her mother. For the first time, she fully manifested the mode of being for herself. This does not mean she no longer needed an object to differentiate, she needed an object available in order to no longer need it.

Therapeutic Regression and the Secret Noncommunicative Self

Unsure if she wanted to speak for herself or for the therapist, she decided that she would say and do nothing in therapy. For a month we sat silently until she became certain that she expressed her own thoughts. In speaking of the treatment of the schizoid patient, Winnicott (1963) states:

> In practice then, there is something we must allow for in our work, the patient's non-communicating as a positive contribution. We must ask ourselves, does our technique allow for the patient to communicate that he or she is not communicating? For this to happen, we as analysts must be ready for the signal: "I am not communicating" and be able to distinguish it from the distress signal associated with a failure of communication. [p. 188]

Estelle grew up in a family in which she was never left alone. Her mother was always present, noisy, domineering and impinging, never letting her be. In the session, she needed to be alone in the presence of the therapist. Her false self had always been manifest in a verbal barrage that protected the silent, noncommunicative core self. No one could know that the true self chose to remain silent. The constant chattering of the false self fooled the outer world into believing that Estelle was always in communication and never alone. When Estelle began to question whether she came to treatment for herself or for others, she said, "I don't know if I want to be here."

Her wording of this statement expressed the basic issue: whether or not she could risk the experience of being in the presence of the other and of silently communicating the wish to be left alone. Estelle and I sat for about a month in a comfortable "silent communication," an experience described by Winnicott (1963) as "therapeutic regression." This phase of treatment is paradoxical in that there is an experience of symbiosis similar to an infant and mother being united without a need for words but also with the sense of being isolated and in solitude. In earliest development, the sense of "continuity-in-being" precedes that of "doing" (Winnicott 1963). The schizoid patient experienced traumatic impingement disrupting the continuity-in-being. Doing is therefore not based on a secure "being" self but instead becomes frantic and compulsive in an effort to compensate for a lack of vitality and spontaneity. Estelle's life was filled with a plenitude of activities, but she always felt unreal, as if she were an automaton. Winnicott (1963) stressed that the therapeutic regression provides the patient with the experience of going-on-being so that desire and doing can be authentically based on a "being" self. In silent communication, the infant or patient creates the subjective object. The therapist's silence permits the patient the omnipotent illusion of creating the subjective object in the transference without the therapist imposing his objectivity on the process. Estelle later said that during the therapeutic regression, she thought of me as existing completely for her, as if I had no life outside of our relationship, and that she and I thought alike about everything. The therapist facilitates the creation of the subjective object by experiencing a primary therapeutic preoccupation toward the patient similar to the mother's primary maternal preoccupation toward the infant. The therapist experiences a corresponding regression in the countertransference comprised of a sense of basic unity with the patient while also vigorously maintaining his professional, observing ego (Grotstein 1985).

Winnicott's description (1963) of the schizoid patient's impaired "being" self is identical to Balint's idea of the basic

fault. The therapeutic regression provides the opportunity fo
reparative work addressing the basic fault. The patient i
provided with a healthy experience of infantile omnipotenc
and the creation of the subjective object in a safe environmen
to provide an authentic basis for separation/individuation.

During the therapeutic regression, the patient is mos
vulnerable in that the secret self, terrified of violation, ha
exposed itself in its need not to communicate and is subject t
psychotic anxieties centering around annihilation. The thera
pist must contain these anxieties and not fail the patient durin
this period. Following the therapeutic regression, the thera
pist's inadvertent and unavoidable mistakes and failures ar
used by the patient in reliving earlier parental failures an
discovering that he can express disappointments and ange
and that the therapeutic relationship and other significan
relationships survive.

Authentic Separation/Individuation

Estelle now felt that she no longer was inclined to be a transi
tional object for the other person. Betty was planning to atten
a wedding and expected to be uncomfortable, given her env
of the bride. She arranged for Estelle to be invited and in
formed Estelle as if she, Betty, were doing Estelle a favor. T
her surprise, Estelle said that she had no interest in the wed
ding. Betty then attempted to persuade her. Estelle expresse
that there were other activities that she would prefer. Estell
then challenged Betty. Estelle said that Betty really wanted he
to go because she needed support. Betty could not own he
own dependency.

This incident was the perfect analogy to Estelle's rela
tionship to her mother, who had denied her own dependenc
on Estelle: mother demanding that Estelle take care of her
Both colluded in denying the mother's dependence. As Estell
became aware of this relational pattern, she first felt enraged a
her mother and Betty but then felt a sorrow, love, and empa
thy. Once it became clear and openly acknowledged by both
that Estelle would go to the wedding because of her relation-

ship with Betty (and for her mother ultimately), Estelle readily volunteered to accompany Betty. Estelle predicted that Betty would probably ignore her altogether at the wedding and she might feel like a fool for going. She said Betty would ignore her to act autonomously and fight off her dependence. I then remarked that it sounded as if Betty needed Estelle's presence in order not to need Estelle. Estelle said that at the wedding she remembered this and did not feel rejected but good about herself for helping Betty. This example illustrates what I noted about how a Fairbairnian point of view aims toward mature dependence in object relations. Estelle's wish to give of herself is not viewed as masochistic or symbiotic but rather as mature object relating. What needed analysis was the former collusion, confusion, and denial of dependence through projective identifications and other defenses. Once the projections are analyzed, Estelle could make her own free choice. This incident also led to the emergence of the heart of the schizoid problem.

The Heart of the Schizoid Problem

Only in advanced stages of the treatment, when the patient's ego is strengthened, does the therapist interpret the dissassociation of the infantile needy self. Estelle had become sufficiently differentiated for the therapist to begin to explore and interpret this issue. Estelle gave evidence of being prepared for this work in her increasing dissatisfaction with the role of transitional object for others. She then became upset since this was the only manner in which she related. The problem raised—if she gave up helping the other she would be isolated—was now occurring. She became hopeless and suicidal. I now began to interpret the empty core, the heart of the treatment of the schizoid patient.

Interpreting the Empty Core

An incident between Estelle and Betty pointed the way toward the interpretation of the empty core. Estelle rarely complained or confided in significant others. As she began to resent being a transitional object, she wanted more for herself. Overwhelmed, Estelle tried to describe to Betty how upset she felt. This was extremely out of character. Betty interrupted her, saying, "How can you complain to me? I should have your problems. I cannot believe that you know all of the problems in my life and you can tell me you are upset about your new job, your boyfriend, and your future."

At first Estelle was devastated. She nearly took her life. Afterward, she decided that she had a right to her feelings. She could not believe that Betty would reject her after all the help she had given Betty. It was the first time she ever cried to Betty about herself. Then she had an even more significant thought: she deserved help not only because she had been there for Betty but simply because she was a person in her own right. It was this thought that reached beyond the bad object, beyond the false self and the fear of abandonment, to the fundamental dilemma of the schizoid position. She confronted both Betty and Betty's cruel response to the plea for help. Betty was not defensive, but to Estelle's surprise, admitted that she was at least partially justified in her feelings. Estelle considered this incident a turning point in the conflict between living and dying.

When she related this incident, I decided that she was emotionally prepared to deal with the empty core. I said, "You have described how your relationships are comprised of you as the giver, fulfilling the needs of an infantile, emotionally starved other. There has always been the question of what has happened to your needs. Now you have begun to express your own dependence, and it is apparent that you have been very sensitive to rejection. I suggest that you have disowned the needy part of yourself and have found it in the infantile, dependent persons you take care of. They represent a hungry, needy part of yourself that you have always had to disown and then you fulfill it by taking care of others who represent it."

Estelle remembered that her mother always conveyed the sense that she was worn out with endless problems and would be completely drained by any demands Estelle made upon her.

I interpreted that Estelle was terrified to express her needs to her mother. She feared her needs could destroy her mother. I said, "You looked into her eyes with your urgent need for love, and you saw her look at you as if you were a vampire. You therefore become terrified of the vampirish, hungry self; you rid yourself of your neediness and instead tried to take care of her dependence. A peculiar thing then occurred. She became the carrier for the needy self, you became the provider. Thus, your mother, who looked at you as if you were a vampire, came to possess your vampirish self."

Estelle now began to associate to the idea of hunger. She recalled that during her years away at college, she had gone through a period of anorexia, eating only soup and vegetables and weighing 90 pounds at 5'4". She was called to the nurse, sent to the university medical center, and her mother had been called in. Not wanting so much attention, she compromised and started to eat an acceptable amount. I interpreted, "Being away from home in college made you become emotionally hungry for your mother. Therefore, you had to take greater measures in repressing the needy self by depriving it of food, a substitute for your mother."

Estelle now was determined not to allow others to completely control her or deny the expression of her needs. She said that the boyfriend she was seeing was narcissistic, did not permit her to talk about herself, and made all plans for their future, which she was not sure she wanted. She described incidents in which he seemed to be destructively competing with her, for example, putting down her new position. He was quite taken with himself as a sexual object, telling her that she was lucky to have him. In truth, she was not attracted to him physically or emotionally. She wanted to tell him this but she thought that maybe she was running away because he was a man. Perhaps she had not separated from her mother and that she should overcome her problems and try to like him. She had the idea that she was working on achieving intimacy with men and that the relationship to this particular man was incidental to pursuing this ideal or goal. Schizoid patients tend to become focused on an abstract idea rather than specific situations, feelings, or desires. In this instance, the actual relationship was perceived only as a means to achieve the ideal of intimacy in the abstract. I emphasized that in the pursuit of relationships she might meet many people she likes and dislikes. She was not obligated to be with any one male because of her goal to achieve intimacy with males. The idea of intimacy could not be abstracted so clearly from the particular relationship it is or is not a quality of. I suggested that if she pursued relationships, she might meet a man she liked more. Fairbairn (1940) stated that schizoid patients often have remarkable psychological insight but it is based on the splitting of the ego. Estelle was able to understand that intimacy was a capacity of the personality but then used this knowledge to approach her relationships scientifically and not personally.

Afterward she reported that she told him how she felt, and especially that he should not plan their future for her. She said that he ceased to be overbearing. When she made it clear that she was a free agent and not obligated to him, she found herself enjoying his company and remembering what she had first liked about him. They therefore continued to see one another but she had more input into the relationship.

The Empty Core Emerging in the Transference

Once I had directly identified for her the empty core of the needy self, I explicitly identified manifestations of it, no matter how disguised, in the transference. The empty core needs to be manifested fully in the transferential situation for it to be resolved. Thus, I focused the treatment on the transference. There had been adequate preparation for this. Previously, I had frequently discussed the internalization or rejection of the therapist as a good object. The therapist may be consciously incorporated as a good holding object but is unconsciously inevitably received as the exciting object.

Estelle would enter treatment and discuss, in detail, her dinner prior to the treatment. I interpreted that she was unconsciously referring to the hunger for the therapist, an emptiness that she filled with food. She accepted this analogy in that she thought of our relationship while she dined. I remarked that she was symbiotically incorporating me. I explained that she was allowing herself to feel the hunger for a good object and to nourish herself with nurturing food. Also there was the fear of the hunger and emptiness transforming the good object into the exciting, frustrating, bad object. In filling herself before the session, she did not have to feel emotionally hungry for me and frustrated during the session.

In the next sessions she was talking about feeling very sexually attracted to a married man she had worked with over many years. She did not understand the suddenness of the attraction and feared she would act out on it. I interpreted that her hunger had now spread from food to sex and that our relationship was creating the hunger for this man. Just as she wanted to fill herself up with food in the outer world so as to avoid hunger and frustration, she also wanted to fill herself with sex in the outside world to avoid the hunger and frustration in therapy. The shift in hunger from food to sex also signified the shift from hunger for the maternal breast to hunger for the paternal oedipal phallus. The fact that the oedipal need is still felt urgently as "hunger" reveals her strong underlying oral need for the mother in the wish for the father.

The following evening, she felt overwhelmed by sexual hunger for me, Betty, and the married lover. I remarked upon the baby's need to be loved as a person in its own right, and when that need is thwarted, the sensual sensations, which are a normal part of the baby's close physical relationship to its parents become increased. Hunger for food and for sexual discharge can replace the hunger for love because they can be self-satisfied and don't have to risk dependence upon the response of the other. These interventions helped Estelle to manage her awakened hunger and emptiness.

She also became aware of separation anxiety and for the first time, as my vacation approached, felt needy and worried about how she would manage on her own. The experience of absolute dependence during the therapeutic regression re-

sulted in Estelle becoming more separate and therefore more
aware of her dependence and separation anxiety. The process
of separation/individuation also occurred in her awareness and
anger over the therapist's mistakes and failures. Estelle spoke
in a detailed, flat, affectless, monotonous manner. Often I was
bored, restless, sleepy, and fidgety in the countertransference.
The patient never seemed to notice my response but related as
if she were talking to a wall. The patient eventually began to
awaken from her lifelessness and to awaken me from my
lethargy by directly commenting that I was especially fidgety
one day. I asked her to tell me about this. Was it just on this
particular day that I was fidgety or was I usually fidgety? What
did she think the reasons were for this?

The patient said that until quite recently, I had never
before been fidgety. It was only lately, in the last weeks, that
she had noticed I seemed sleepy and tired, and at other times
restless. I asked her to tell me all about my sleepiness. Did I
look as if I had fallen completely asleep, that I was drifting off,
but catching myself, that I was snoring? Could she tell me
about what she saw, how she felt, what she made of it?

She said I looked sleepy, as if I had begun to drift off (she
rolled her eyes in imitation) then caught myself and quietly or
unobtrusively shook myself awake. She thought I might be
tired because I was very busy these days, I was up late the
evening before, or because I was bored and tired of her. She
did not believe that I was bored with her, but she was not
certain. She then laughed and remarked that I no longer looked
fidgety or sleepy; I was wide awake and "with it." She had
awakened me.

In the treatment of this patient, I had actually been bored,
restless, and lethargic all along. Her periodic suicidal crises
would awaken me from my chronic lethargy. The patient had
never before noticed me enough as a person to notice my
response to listening to her. It was actually an indication that
she was coming alive emotionally that she noticed me to be
more than the woodwork. It is interesting to note that a year
before, I could never have pictured her noticing or commenting on my reaction. As I looked back upon the previous

sessions, I realized that she began to notice my dead (tired) state after I had interpreted the emotional deadness in her relationship to her mother. She had never been a bother to her mother. She was beginning to come alive by becoming a "bother" and awakening me. Up until that time, she always came to sessions on time or slightly late, but never early. As soon as I glanced at the clock to say the time was up, she was out of her seat to leave. I always thought of her as not being a bother. In her nonverbal conduct, in her tone and in her gestures, she communicated, "I am not a bother, so love me and don't abandon me." In my mind, I would sometimes compare her to my demanding borderline patients and wish that they were less of a bother, more like Estelle. I had actually taken on the countertransferential position of the mother, who had often compared the demanding older sister to quiet, well-behaved Estelle. She confronted me with how I failed her and demanded that I remain emotionally alive and awake. In this way, she was separating from and curing the depressive bad object.

Estelle continued to function well in her job and in her relationships. She became aware that most of her frantic, compulsive activity served to shield the fragile, regressed self. As she internalized a supportive relationship, she began to feel a foundation to her personality. She sorted out what she does that is for herself and what she does that is for others. It became important for her not to feel used by others or to do for others what they could do for themselves. She became tired of her bureaucratic job and thought she might want to do something that would be creative and provide more contact with people.

This book has described the object relations theory of schizoid states along with ensuing therapeutic strategies. The independent tradition of British object relations theory has considered the schizoid position as the foundation of psychic structure. Fairbairn's concept of an original pristine, unitary self suggests that the infant is born with an innate striving potential to develop its individuality. The primary love associated with good-enough object relations is as essential for the infant's individuation as oxygen is for biological survival. The pursuit of individuation proves to be a difficult struggle and is manifested in the child's gradual efforts to differentiate from the symbiotic identification with the internal object.

In normative, adaptive development, the schizoid position provides the child the opportunity for internalization, differentiation, and the development of inner resources. In pathological schizoid states, the individual lives primarily in the mind, relating to the internal object world, because a vulnerable self has given up on receiving primary love from the external object world and instead expects only impingement from persecutory objects. The original lack of primary love is experienced as emptiness. The hunger for object love is transformed into an empty core, which is filled with part object relationships. In this sense, part objects may be understood as signifiers of the lack of primary love.

The essence of the schizoid position is that the child transfers his relationships with external objects to the inner realm. The schizoid position serves separation/individuation by enabling the child to become less dependent upon the external world. In pathological schizoid states, the outer world derives its meaning almost exclusively from the inner world. Schizoid individuals may construct intellectual systems as love objects at the expense of human relationships. Assuming a Rousseauian perspective, Fairbairn believed that our modern, highly technological civilization and its alienation from nature and natural human relationships was itself schizoid. He pointed out the catastrophic effect schizoid pathology has had during this century. For instance, when a deeply schizoid individual falls in love with an extreme political ideology, the consequences may be devastating in the toll of human lives. The schizoid person may feel that the joy of loving is forever out of his reach since he has come to believe that his love is destructive. Utilizing prescientific, theological language, Fairbairn says that the schizoid person may thereby make a pact with the devil, stating, "Evil be thou my good." Since loving involves destroying, it is better to destroy by hate, which is intrinsically destructive, than to destroy by love, which is inherently good and creative. This tie to the bad object fulfills the longing of the schizoid individual's empty core.

References

Atwood, G., and Stolorow, R. (1984). *Structures of Subjectivity.* Hillsdale, NJ: The Analytic Press.

Balint, M. (1968). *The Basic Fault: Therapeutic Aspects of Regression.* New York: Brunner/Mazel.

Barrett, W. (1986). *Death of the Soul.* New York: Doubleday.

Binswanger, L. (1944). The case of Ellen West. In *Existence,* ed. R. May, pp. 237–364. New York: Basic Books, 1958.

_____ (1963). *Being-in-the-World.* New York: Basic Books.

Bion, W. (1962). *Learning from Experience.* London: Maresfield Library Reprints.

_____ (1967). *Second Thoughts.* London: Maresfield Library.

Bollas, C. *The Shadow of the Object.* New York: Columbia University Press.

Buber, M. (1958). *I and Thou.* New York: Scribners.

Chess, S. (1970). Temperament and children at risk. In *The Child in His Family,* ed. E. J. Antony, and C. Koupernik, pp. 121–130. New York: John Wiley and Sons.

Chodorow, N. (1989). *Feminism and Psychoanalytic Theory.* New Haven, CT: Yale University Press.

Derrida, J. (1978). *Writing and Difference.* Chicago, IL: University of Chicago Press.

Eco, U. (1984). *Semiotics and the Philosophy of Language.* Bloomington, IN: Indiana University Press.

References

Eigen, M. (1986). *The Psychotic Core.* Northvale, NJ: Jason Aronson.

Ellenberger, H. F. (1958). A clinical introduction to psychiatric phenomenology and existential analysis. In *Existence,* ed. R. May, E. Angel, and H. F. Ellenberger, pp. 237–364. New York: Basic Books.

Fairbairn, W. R. D. (1929). The relationship of dissociation and depression, considered from the point of view of medical psychology. [M.D. thesis] Edinburgh University, unpublished.

———— (1940). Schizoid factors in the personality. In *Psychoanalytic Studies of the Personality,* pp. 3–27. London: Routledge and Kegan Paul, 1981.

———— (1941). A revised psychopathology of the psychoses and psychoneurosis. In *Psychoanalytic Studies of the Personality,* pp. 28–58. London: Routledge and Kegan Paul, 1981.

———— (1943). The repression and return of bad objects. In *Psychoanalytic Studies of the Personality,* pp. 58–81. London: Routledge and Kegan Paul, 1981.

———— (1944). Endopsychic structure considered in terms of object-relationships. In *Psychoanalytic Studies of the Personality,* pp. 82–136. London: Routledge and Kegan Paul, 1981.

———— (1946). Object relationships and dynamic structure. In *Psychoanalytic Studies of the Personality,* pp. 137–151. London: Routledge and Kegan Paul, 1981.

———— (1949). Steps in the development of an object relations theory of personality. In *Psychoanalytic Studies of the Personality,* pp. 152–161. London: Routledge and Kegan Paul, 1981.

———— (1951). A synopsis of the development of the author's views regarding the structure of the personality. In *Psychoanalytic Studies of the Personality,* pp. 162–182. London: Routledge and Kegan Paul, 1981.

Freud, S. (1925). Negation. In *Collected Papers,* vol. 5, pp. 181–185. New York: Basic Books, 1959.

———— (1929). *Civilization and Its Discontents.* New York: W. W. Norton.

———— (1937). Analysis terminable and interminable. In *Collected Papers,* vol. 5, pp. 316–357. London: Basic Books, 1959.

———— (1949). *An Outline of Psychoanalysis.* New York: Norton.

Giovacchini, P. (1986). *Developmental Disorders.* Northvale, NJ: Jason Aronson.

Grolnick, S. (1990). *The Work and Play of Winnicott.* Northvale, NJ: Jason Aronson.

Grosskurth, P. (1986). *Melanie Klein: Her World and Her Work.* Cambridge, MA: Harvard University Press, 1987.

Grotstein, J. (1985). *Splitting and Projective Identification.* Northvale, NJ: Jason Aronson.

Guntrip, H. (1969). *Schizoid Phenomena, Object Relations and the Self.* New York: International Universities Press.

Hartmann, H. (1950). *Essays on Ego Psychology*. New York: International Universities Press, 1964.

Hegel, G. W. F. (1807). *Phenomenology of Spirit*. London: Oxford University Press, 1977.

Heidegger, M. (1927). Dasein's possibility of being-a-whole and being-towards-death. In *Being and Time*, pp. 279–311. New York: Harper and Row, 1962.

Jacobson, E. (1964). Narcissism, masochism, and the concepts of self and self representations. In *The Self and the Object World*, pp. 3–23. New York: International Universities Press.

Kafka, F. (1971). A hunger artist. In *The Complete Stories*, ed. N. N. Glatzer, pp. 268–277. New York: Schocken.

Kierkegaard, S. (1949). *The Sicknesses Unto Death*. Princeton, NJ: Princeton University Press, 1980.

Klein, M. (1926). The psychological principles of early analysis. In *Love, Guilt and Reparation and Other Works*, pp. 128–138. New York: The Free Press, 1975.

_____ (1929). Personification in the play of children. In *Love, Guilt and Reparation and Other Works*, pp. 199–209. New York: The Free Press, 1975.

_____ (1930). The importance of symbol-formation in the development of the ego. In *Love, Guilt and Reparation and Other Works*, pp. 219–232. New York: The Free Press, 1975.

_____ (1935). A contribution to the psychogenesis of manic-depressive states. In *Love, Guilt and Reparation and Other Works*, pp. 262–287. New York: The Free Press, 1975.

_____ (1946). Notes on some schizoid mechanisms. In *Development in Psychoanalysis*, ed. J. Riviere, pp. 1–24. London: Hogarth Press, 1952.

Kohut, H. (1971). *The Analysis of the Self*. New York: International Universities Press.

_____ (1977). *The Restoration of the Self*. New York: International Universities Press.

_____ (1984). *How Does Analysis Cure?* Chicago, IL: University of Chicago Press.

Lacan, J. (1949). *Ecrits*. New York: W. W. Norton, 1977.

_____ (1988). *The Seminar of Jacques Lacan*. New York: W. W. Norton.

Laing, R. D. (1959). *The Divided Self*. Middlesex: Penguin.

Little, M. I. (1986). On basic unity. In *The British School of Psychoanalysis: The Independent Tradition*, ed. G. Kohon, pp. 136–153. London: Free Association Books.

_____ (1990). *Psychotic Anxieties and Containment: A Personal Record of an Analysis with Winnicott*. Northvale, NJ: Jason Aronson.

Loewald, H. (1972). Freud's conception of the negative therapeutic reaction, with comments on instinct theory. In *Papers on Psychoanalysis*, pp. 315–325. New Haven, CT: Yale University Press, 1980.

―――― (1973). On internalization. In *Papers on Psychoanalysis*, pp. 69–86. New Haven, CT: Yale University Press, 1980.

Mahler, M., Pine, F., and Bergman, A. (1975). *The Psychological Birth of the Human Infant.* New York: Basic Books.

Masterson, J. (1976). *The Clinical Picture: A Developmental Perspective.* New York: Brunner/Mazel.

May, R. (1983). *The Discovery of Being.* New York: W. W. Norton.

Meissner, W. (1988). *Treatment of Patients in the Borderline Spectrum.* Northvale, NJ: Jason Aronson.

Ogden, T. (1989). *The Primitive Edge of Experience.* Northvale, NJ: Jason Aronson.

Rousseau, J.-J. (1762). *The Social Contract and Discourses.* London: Everyman's Library, 1973.

Sartre, J.-P. (1943). *Being and Nothingness.* New York: Washington Square Press, 1956.

―――― (1984). *The War Diaries of Jean-Paul Sartre: November 1939 to March 1940.* New York: Pantheon.

Schoenewolf, G. (1990a). *Turning Points in Analytic Therapy: The Classic Cases.* Northvale, NJ: Jason Aronson.

―――― (1990b). *Turning Points in Analytic Therapy: From Kernberg to Winnicott.* Northvale, NJ: Jason Aronson.

Searles, H. (1962). The differentiation between concrete and metaphorical thinking in the recovering schizophrenic patient. In *Collected Papers on Schizophrenia and Related Subjects*, pp. 250–283. New York: International Universities Press, 1965.

―――― (1986). *My Work with Borderline Patients.* Northvale, NJ: Jason Aronson.

Seinfeld, J. (1990). *The Bad Object: Handling the Negative Therapeutic Reaction in Psychotherapy.* Northvale, NJ: Jason Aronson.

Sophocles. Oedipus at Colonus. In *The Theban Plays.* New York: Penguin, 1982.

Sours, J. A. (1980). *Starving to Death in a Sea of Objects: The Anorexia Nervosa Syndrome.* New York: Jason Aronson.

Spitz, R. (1965). *The First Year of Life.* New York: International Universities Press.

Stern, D. (1985). *The Interpersonal World of the Infant.* New York: Basic Books.

Storr, A. (1988). *Churchill's Black Dog, Kafka's Mice.* New York: Ballantine Books.

Sutherland, J. (1989). *Fairbairn's Journey into the Interior.* London: Free Association Books.

Volkan, V. (1987). *Six Steps in the Treatment of the Borderline Personality Organization.* Northvale, NJ: Jason Aronson.

Wilson, A. (1988). *Tolstoy.* New York: Fawcett Columbine.

Wilson, C. P. (1986). Ego functioning in psychosomatic disorders. In *Psychosomatic Symptoms: Psychodynamic Treatment of the Underlying Personality Disorder,* ed. C. P. Wilson and I. L. Mintz, pp. 13–32. Northvale, NJ: Jason Aronson, 1989.

Winnicott, D. W. (1936). Appetite and emotional disorder. In *Through Paediatrics to Psychoanalysis,* pp. 33–51. London: Hogarth Press, 1978.

_____ (1945). Primitive emotional development. In *Through Paediatrics to Psycho-analysis,* pp. 145–156. London: Hogarth Press, 1978.

_____ (1947). Hate in the counter-transference. In *Through Paediatrics to Psycho-analysis,* pp. 194–203. London: Hogarth Press, 1978.

_____ (1951). Transitional objects and transitional phenomena. In *Through Pae-diatrics to Psychoanalysis,* pp. 229–242. London: Hogarth Press, 1978.

_____ (1954). The depressive position in normal development. In *Through Pae-diatrics to Psychoanalysis,* pp. 262–277. London: Hogarth Press, 1978.

_____ (1956). The anti-social tendency. In *Through Paediatrics to Psychoanalysis,* pp. 306–315. London, Hogarth Press, 1978.

_____ (1960). Ego distortion in terms of true and false self. In *The Maturational Process and the Facilitating Environment,* pp. 140–152. New York: International Universities Press, 1965.

_____ (1962). The aims of psychoanalytic treatment. In *The Maturational Processes and the Facilitating Environment,* pp. 166–170. New York: International Universities Press, 1965.

_____ (1963). Communicating and not communicating leading to a study of certain opposites. In *The Maturational Processes and the Facilitating Environment,* pp. 179–192. New York: International Universities Press, 1965.

_____ (1971). *Playing and Reality.* London: Tavistock.

Index

251

(Bridge Lake)

Anne-Micke   Hans Terline

R.R.I   Lone Butte B.

V0K 1X0

604-
593-4603
395-3659